Mapp v. Ohio
Evidence and Search Warrants

Deborah A. Persico

Landmark Supreme Court Cases

Enslow Publishers, Inc.

44 Fadem Road	PO Box 38
Box 699	Aldershot
Springfield, NJ 07081	Hants GU12 6BP
USA	UK

Library of Congress Cataloging-in-Publication Data

Persico, Deborah A.
    Mapp v. Ohio: evidence and search warrants / Deborah A. Persico.
        p. cm. — (Landmark Supreme Court cases)
    Includes bibliographical references and index.
    Summary: The landmark Supreme Court case that dealt with drawing
the line between legal and illegal searches of private residences and
what evidence obtained from such searches is admissible in court.
    ISBN 0-89490-857-X
    1. Mapp, Dollree—Trials, litigation, etc.—Juvenile literature.
2. Exclusionary rule (Evidence)—United States—Juvenile literature.
[1. Mapp, Dollree. 2. Exclusionary rule (Evidence)] I. Title. II. Series
KF224.M213P47   1997
345.73'0522—dc20
[347.305522]
                                   96-21295
                                   CIP
                                   AC

Printed in the United States of America

10 9 8 7 6 5 4 3 2 1

Dedication

This book is dedicated to my husband and best friend, Joseph, whose encouragement, creativity, and sense of humor make life so much easier, and to my parents, Ralph and Lena, whose youthful energy has always been a source of inspiration.

Acknowledgments

The author would like to offer special thanks to:

Joseph Virgilio, Esquire, my husband, for tireless hours of help in preparing this manuscript.

Bill Saks, Esquire, and Chris Link, Esquire, of the Ohio office of the American Civil Liberties Union, for helping me locate background information on the *Mapp* case.

Dollree Mapp, for her personal insight.

Carl Delau, for providing photographs and his personal insight into the case.

Dorothy Flaherty, my good friend and neighbor, for her kind encouragement.

Contents

1

The Right to Be Secure in Your Home

On May 23, 1957, at about 1:30 P.M., three police officers from the Cleveland Police Department arrived at 14705 Milverton Street in Cleveland, Ohio. It was the home of Dollree "Dolly" Mapp, the former spouse of light heavyweight world boxing champion, Jimmy Bivans. Mapp, then thirty-two years old, lived alone with her thirteen-year-old daughter, Barbara Bivans, on the second floor of the two-family brick house. Barbara was not at home at the time.

The officers rang the doorbell and Dolly Mapp came to the window and asked what they wanted. They said they wanted to come inside to question her but they would not give her any details. The truth was that they were investigating a recent bombing and suspected that a man named Virgil Ogletree, who they believed had information about the bombing, was hiding inside the house. The bombing incident and the cast of characters involved in it would form a curious backdrop to the court proceedings to come.

The events leading up to the police visit to the Mapp home had begun three days earlier on May 20, 1957, at 3:00 A.M., when a bomb exploded on the front porch of the home of Donald "The Kid" King.[1] King, who is now a famous promoter of championship boxing bouts, was known then to the police as a clearinghouse operator, a person who runs a business where illegal gambling bets are placed and the winners are paid. In a highly unusual move, King went to the police for help.

According to an article published in the local newspaper, the *Cleveland Plain Dealer*, King made history when he told Sergeant Carl J. Delau about a notorious gang of Cleveland gambling racketeers.[2] Apparently, a man named Shondor Birns had been involved in a shakedown racket of five clearinghouse operators.[3] Birns had persuaded each operator, including King, to pay him two hundred dollars a week to keep peace among the operators.[4] Two men known as enforcers or musclemen helped Birns collect his money.

8

5 Now Held in Bombing of King's Home

Boone Gives Up; Birns Already in Jail

BULLETIN

Daniel Boone, 46, sought in the bombing early yesterday of Donald King, surrendered to police here last night. He denied any knowledge of the bombing.

The back alleys of the numbers game were being swept clean last night as police searched for two missing suspects in the bombing of Donald (the Kid) King's home.

Four others, including Shondor Birns, again No. 1 on the police roster of racketeers, were already jailed and held for questioning.

King, 25-year-old clearinghouse operator, and his common-law wife, Luevania Henderson, signed statements and were released with a police guard to their bomb-blasted home, 3713 E. 151st Street.

Police Chief Frank W. Story refused King permission to carry a gun but took steps to provide him around-the-clock protection.

The cast of characters in the bombing plot investigation as reported by Detective Lt. Martin P. Cooney and Sgt. Carl Delau of the racket squad, includes five clearinghouse operators, two musclemen and Birns.

All have police records.

The operators include King; Edward Keeling, 31, 2493 E. 83rd Street; Thomas Turk, 1507 E. 107th Street; Willie (Buck-

*(Continued on Page 14, Column 4)

Shondor Birns
Questioned

Donald (The Kid) King
Home bombed

Pair Sought in Bombing of King's Home

★ From First Page

eye) Jackson, 54, of 1497 E. 108th Street, and Dan Boone, 46, of 1613 E. 115th Street.

The musclemen were said to be Samson Powell, 36, of 2329 E. 97th Street, a former heavyweight Golden Glover, and Elijah Abercrombie, 41, of 1471 E. 112th Street.

Boone and Abercrombie were the two still sought.

According to police, Powell and Abercrombie are "enforcers" for Birns. Abercrombie was also described as the "money pickup man" who delivered Birns' share of clearinghouse take.

Tells Police All

King made history yesterday when he openly turned to police with information he said would help send someone to jail.

His story as told to Sgt. Delau placed Birns in the middle of clearinghouse operations and implicated Birns in a shakedown racket.

Apparently Birns entered the numbers field last October, shortly after he completed a 26-month prison stay for income tax evasion, Delau said.

Birns was either invited by the numbers men or he "persuaded" them to accept his services to keep peace among them and hold payoff odds to the same level of about 400 or 500 to one, Delau said he believed.

$1,000 Weekly

King told police the price for Birns' services as chairman of the board was $200 a week from each of the five operators. Abercrombie collected the $200 weekly at their homes, he said.

In December, King said, he cut his payments to Birns to $100 and in February stopped

---

When police visited Dolly Mapp's home on May 23, 1957, they were investigating a recent bombing at the home of Donald "The Kid" King. They suspected that a man named Virgil Ogletree, who they believed had information about the bombing, was hiding inside Dolly Mapp's house.

King told Sargeant Delau that in December 1956 he had decided to cut his payments to Birns in half. Then, in February 1957, King stopped paying altogether. Birns called him repeatedly and accused King of not fulfilling his obligations. King still refused to pay. On May 20, a bomb exploded on King's front porch.

Within twenty-four hours after the bombing, police had detained four men, including Shondor Birns, for questioning. The police had also received a telephone tip that Virgil Ogletree was connected with the bombing and that he was hiding at Dolly Mapp's home. In addition to that tip, the informant had also told the police that Mapp's house was the infamous "California Gold" policy house, a clearinghouse for gambling bets, where the police could expect to find plenty of policy paraphernalia—in other words, gambling slips and records.[5] It was for those reasons that Sergeant Carl Delau and Officers Thomas Devers and Michael Haney went to Mapp's home on May 23, 1957.

When the police refused to tell her why they were there, Mapp said she wanted to contact her attorney. If the attorney said it was all right to let them in, then she would do so.

Dolly Mapp tried to reach Alexander L. Kearns, an attorney who was handling a civil lawsuit that she had filed against her ex-boyfriend, Archie Moore, also a light heavyweight world boxing champion. Kearns was in court at the time but his partner, Walter L. Greene, told Mapp not to let the police officers inside unless they showed her a search warrant and allowed her to read it.

Dolly Mapp told the police officers waiting outside what Greene had said. They did not show her a search warrant so Mapp would not let them come inside. But the officers did not leave. They continued to wait outside the home for the next three hours.

At about 4:30 P.M., at least four more police officers arrived at Mapp's residence. Walter Greene also arrived, just in time to see one of the officers attempting to kick in the door. When Mapp still would not let them in, a police officer broke the glass in the door and reached inside to unlock it so the other officers could enter.

As the police burst into her home, Dolly Mapp was descending the stairs from the second floor to the front door. She demanded to see a search warrant. One of the officers held up a piece of paper and said, "Here is the search warrant," but when Mapp asked to see it, he refused to show it to her.[6]

Determined to see the warrant, Mapp grabbed the piece of paper from the officer's hand and shoved it down the front of her dress. The officer grabbed her, reached into her dress, and removed the paper. Then, he twisted her hand behind her back and handcuffed her to himself. Mapp yelled and pleaded with him to turn her loose.[7]

Walter Greene, the attorney, had tried to follow the police officers inside Mapp's home, but the officers prevented him from entering or speaking with Mapp. He heard Dolly Mapp call out several times, but each time he asked to be allowed in the residence an officer told him he could not go inside.

While the police fanned out through the house searching the kitchen, the living room, the basement, and rooms on the second floor, one officer forcibly led Mapp upstairs to her bedroom. This was a room she had recently moved into after a previous boarder had moved out. She sat handcuffed on the bed and watched as two officers searched the dresser, chest of drawers, and her suitcase. Greene, who was still waiting outside, heard "a great deal of commotion and loud talk" coming from inside the house.[8]

During the widespread search, the police officers discovered a gun and several obscene books, photographs, and a pencil sketch. Mapp told the officers that the items did not belong to her, but they ignored her. They also found a trunkful of policy slips, that is, the records of gambling bets. The police confiscated all of the items and placed Dolly Mapp under arrest.

Police burst into the Cleveland, Ohio, home of Dolly Mapp on May 23, 1957. When Mapp demanded to see a search warrant, one of the officers held up a piece of paper. Mapp never did get to see an actual search warrant, however.

Virgil Ogletree, the man the police wanted for questioning, was inside the house as police suspected. He had "sneaked down the back stairs" and police found him in an apartment on the first floor.[9] The woman who lived in that apartment told police that he had threatened her. Greene watched as the police led Mapp and Ogletree out of the house.

At the Central Police Station, the police questioned Virgil Ogletree and released him. He was not charged in connection with the bombing. Dolly Mapp did not get off so easily. Sergeant Delau questioned her and then charged her with possession of the gambling paraphernalia and obscene materials. At the time, possession of pornographic or obscene materials was illegal in Ohio. Neither Mapp nor her attorney, Greene, were ever permitted to see the search warrant.

The charge for possession of gambling paraphernalia was a misdemeanor, meaning that it was a less serious charge handled by a court known as the police court. Dolly Mapp went to trial on that charge and was acquitted, that is, she was found not guilty.

Dolly Mapp at first pleaded guilty to the charge of possession of obscene material, but she later withdrew her guilty plea and entered a plea of not guilty. Although she was arrested in May 1957, her trial would not begin until September 3, 1958.

CRIMINAL RECORD DEPARTMENT
CRIMINAL COURTS BUILDING

6 832 6

Dollree Mapp

No. **68436**   Name **Mapp, Dolly** (Dollree Mapp)   Alias

Offense **Possession Obscene Literature**   G. C. **2905.34**

Home Address **4786 Lee. Road** - *14705 MILVERTON - U.P.*   Term **$200 -$2000** or not more **7 yrs**

Occupation **Designer**   File No. **34912**

Business Address.   Arrest Date **5-25-57**

Date of Birth **10-30-24**   Bail: **5,000 2,500**

City and State of Birth **Austin, Texas**

Nativity **Am.**   Race **Negro**   M Div. **S**   M   Female Age **28 33**

Arrested By: **Dever 990, Haney 258, Murphy, Tolan**

Auto License **AK-2908**   Driver's License **NG**   Prob. No. **21708**

B. O. **D-6-25-57**   G. J. **9-17-57**   Indt. **9-19-57** Argmt. **9-20-57** Trial Prob. **7-8-58**

Accomplices

Change plea to guilty-7-8-58. Withdraw guilty plea & plea not guilty-
Disposition **same bail-8-1-58. Indictment amended to indicate deft's**
correct name Dollree Mapp-Jury, imp & sworn-on trial-progress-9-3-58.
Verdict guilty-9-4-58. MNTO 9-8-58. Entry of 9-8-58 vacated to give
deft. opportunity to argue motion-Deft. Sent.O.S.Reformatory for Women
MNTO (Jury-58) of 9-10-58 Motion for stay of execution granted-on
appeal

Judge **Donald F. Lybarger**   Date Sentenced **9-11-58**

Photo No.   Institutional No.

A copy of the Criminal Record Department document listing the charge against Dolly Mapp is shown here. Mapp was charged with possession of gambling paraphernalia and obscene materials. At the time, possession of pornographic or obsence materials was illegal in Ohio.

What would happen at Dolly Mapp's trial? Would the obscene material be introduced as evidence against her? Would it matter that the police did not show her a search warrant? Did the police really have a search warrant?

The United States Supreme Court would become interested in Dolly Mapp's case—but why? How would the decision of the Supreme Court begin to affect every police search and seizure in the country for many years to come?

In order to fully answer these questions, we need to travel back in time to the eighteenth century and meet for a moment with our country's founding fathers.

2

History of the Exclusionary Rule

The right of the people to be secure in their persons, houses, papers, and effects, against unreasonable searches and seizures, shall not be violated; and no Warrants shall issue, but upon probable cause, supported by Oath or affirmation, and particularly describing the place to be searched, and the persons or things to be seized.[1]

The year was 1789. An intense struggle had been raging for the preceding two years between the Republic's two leading political parties, the Anti-Federalists and the Federalists, over the content of the Constitution that was submitted for approval to the First Congress on September 17, 1787: The Constitution did not include a Bill of Rights.[2]

The Anti-Federalists insisted on a Bill of Rights. They were also opposed to the power the Constitution placed in the hands of the president. The Federalists, on the other hand, were not totally opposed to including a Bill of Rights and agreed to do so when the First Congress assembled. This took away some of the Anti-Federalists' steam and eventually made ratification, or approval, of the Constitution much easier for the states.[3]

Virginian James Madison, a member of the House of Representatives, was a staunch supporter of the Constitution and leader of the effort to draft a Bill of Rights. On June 8, 1789, he introduced a list of proposed amendments to the Constitution.[4] In order to compile a Bill of Rights he thought the states would be more likely to approve, Madison looked to the individual state constitutions for guidance, especially the one in his home state of Virginia.[5] Virginia had been the first state to condemn the use of general search warrants and arrest warrants, that is, warrants that did not "describe in detail the places to be searched and the persons or things to be seized."[6] During the time when the states were still colonies subject to the law of England, general warrants were commonly used by English royal officers to enter and search any house, shop, or ship and seize any goods that they thought were evidence of smuggling of unlicensed goods of any kind, including publications. The general warrant allowed an officer to enter a person's home by breaking the door down and to open any closed containers, like boxes, closets, trunks, or drawers, to search for evidence. After the colonies declared their independence from England, Virginia's constitution outlawed the use of general search warrants.

One of Madison's proposed amendments followed the Virginia Bill of Rights. It provided for the right against unreasonable searches and seizures, thus guaranteeing personal security to every citizen. The proposal Madison submitted was almost identical to the words we now know as the Fourth Amendment to the Constitution of the United States.

James Madison's list of proposed amendments also contained a clause stating that no person shall be required to be a witness against oneself—in other words, to accuse oneself of a crime or make oneself appear guilty of a crime. The states would want their new federal constitution to grant each citizen the privilege against self-incrimination.

The states' concern stemmed from a thirteenth-century court procedure called the oath *ex officio*. The procedure was popular in church tribunals, also known as ecclesiastical courts, that existed at the time. During

James Madison (shown here) proposed a Bill of Rights be added to the Constitution. One of Madison's proposed amendments to the Constitution provided for the right against unreasonable searches and seizures. This, Madison felt, would guarantee personal security to each citizen.

the oath *ex officio*, a defendant could be forced, by torture if necessary, to answer any questions the court had, even if the answers incriminated the defendant.[7] Four centuries later, during the 1600s, many people began to protest the oath *ex officio*. In 1641, the Massachusetts Body of Liberties finally prohibited the use of torture as a means of obtaining evidence against a defendant. At the same time, the practice was abolished in England. Then, in 1776, Virginia became the first state to guarantee the privilege against self-incrimination through its state constitution.

James Madison's proposal to include the privilege against self-incrimination in the Bill of Rights is now contained in the Fifth Amendment to the Constitution of the United States: *No person shall . . . be compelled in any criminal case to be witness against himself. . . .*

As the Fourth and Fifth Amendments were being drafted in 1789, James Madison predicted that courts would naturally be inclined to resist every encroachment or infringement upon the rights listed in the Bill of Rights.[8] More than one hundred years later, about seventy-five years before the police forcibly entered Dolly Mapp's home in Ohio, James Madison's prediction became a reality. In the case of *Boyd* v. *United States*, the Supreme Court interpreted the Fourth Amendment right of privacy and the Fifth Amendment right against self-incrimination as applying to all government invasions of "the sanctity of a man's home and the privacies of life."[9]

Unlike the circumstances in Mapp's case, though, *Boyd* v. *United States* did not involve a forced police entry onto premises and the seizure of evidence. Rather, federal agents obtained a court order requiring the defendant to turn over to the court his private accounting books, invoices, and records. The agents believed those documents would prove that the defendant had fraudulently, using dishonest means, imported certain goods into this country.

The federal government argued that the court order did not amount to a "search and seizure" under the Fourth Amendment, because the federal agents did not forcibly enter the defendant's home to search for his papers. The Supreme Court disagreed. It held that because the court order compelled the production of documents, meaning that the defendant had no choice but to comply with the order, it did amount to an unreasonable search and seizure under the Fourth Amendment. But it was not only the Fourth Amendment that the Supreme Court was concerned about. Justice Joseph P. Bradley, who wrote the *Boyd* opinion, also noted that when the federal government orders a person to turn over evidence that may incriminate him or her, it is actually compelling the person to become a witness against himself—clearly violating the Fifth Amendment privilege against self-incrimination. Justice Bradley used the "intimate relation between the two amendments" to justify finding that the order for Mr. Boyd to produce his own documents was unconstitutional.[10]

But what exactly had the *Boyd* Court meant when it said that the constitutional amendments applied to all *government* invasions of privacy? Was it referring to state governments as well as the federal government? What would happen if a private citizen invaded another individual's right of privacy? And, most importantly, what was the appropriate remedy for a violation of a defendant's constitutional rights?

It would be quite some time before the Supreme Court would be given the opportunity to develop answers to those questions.

Before considering several other cases that formed the stepping stones to Dolly Mapp's case, take special note that the *Boyd* case involved *federal* agents charging a violation of *federal* law in a *federal* court. What is significant about those facts? The answer begins with an explanation of the differences between federal law and state law.

Whenever a person commits a crime, he or she violates either federal law or state law; in many cases, he or she may be violating both sets of laws at the same time. Federal criminal laws, which are contained in a series of volumes called the United States Code, are enacted or passed into law by Congress on Capitol Hill in Washington, D.C. Examples of some crimes that federal criminal laws address are espionage (spying), income tax evasion, destruction of national defense materials, violation of immigration laws, and stowing away on vessels or aircraft. Examples of crimes subject to state criminal laws, which are enacted by the individual state legislatures, are possession of illegal narcotics, armed robbery, assault, and murder.

In many cases, though, certain crimes are covered under both state law and federal law. For example, distribution of a large quantity of illegal narcotics is both a state crime (in the state where the crime was committed) and a federal crime. Prosecutors (also called district attorneys) are the attorneys who enforce state law. United States attorneys are the attorneys who enforce federal law. They may jointly decide whether a defendant will be prosecuted in state court or in federal court. Often, that will depend on which law, state or federal, provides for a more severe penalty for the crime charged.

Crimes such as kidnapping, fraud, and auto theft, which are usually prosecuted in state courts, become federal crimes when the defendant crosses state lines. Also, if a person commits a crime on federal property, the case will usually be prosecuted in federal court. Examples of federal property are national parks and military installations.

This distinction between federal law and state law is critical to understanding why Dolly Mapp's case was so important. The *Boyd* decision dealt only with the effects of the Fourth and Fifth Amendments in federal cases. But Mapp's case involved city police officers charging a violation of state law in a state court. How, then, would it be that Mapp's case would reach the Supreme Court?

In 1914, twenty-nine years after *Boyd*, the Supreme Court still seemed determined to apply the Fourth and Fifth Amendments to federal cases only. In the case of *Weeks* v. *United States*, the Supreme Court specifically stated so.[11] Justice William R. Day, writing the opinion for the Court, stated that the limitations of the Fourth Amendment reach only "the Federal Government and its agencies."[12] Fortunately for Fremont Weeks, it was a federal marshal who entered his home without either a search warrant or the consent of Weeks, who was not there, and confiscated papers that were then used to convict him of a federal offense in a federal court in Missouri. The trial court allowed the government to use that evidence. The Supreme Court, however, ruled that the tactics of the federal agent violated Mr. Weeks's rights under the Fourth and Fifth Amendments to the Constitution.

The *Weeks* Court based its decision on the fundamentals of the Fourth Amendment—the idea that "a man's house was his castle and not to be invaded by any general authority to search and seize his goods and papers."[13] It distinguished *unreasonable* searches, which the Fourth Amendment prohibited, from those searches that were legal. For example, it is legal for a police officer without a warrant to search a person under arrest and the area within that person's immediate control, or close reach, for evidence of a crime. It is also legal for a police officer to search a person or that person's property if the person voluntarily consents to the search. For an officer to enter a person's home without a valid search warrant specifically describing the places to be searched and things to be seized, as the federal officer had done in Fremont Weeks's home, was quite a different matter.

But how should the Supreme Court remedy a violation of the Fourth Amendment? The Supreme Court's reasoning boiled down to this: If evidence wrongfully seized could be used against a defendant at trial, then the Fourth Amendment "is of no value, and, so far as those thus placed are concerned, might as well be stricken from the Constitution."[14] The remedy seemed clear to the *Weeks* Court. It held that evidence that is seized by federal law enforcement officers in violation of a defendant's constitutional rights is inadmissible—it cannot be used—against a defendant in a federal trial court. The rule became known as the exclusionary rule.

What exactly did the Court mean when it ruled that evidence was inadmissible? It meant that during a defendant's trial in federal court, the prosecutor would not be permitted to show the evidence to the jury (if the evidence was a document or something else that was tangible). The prosecutor also could not tell the jury about the evidence, either through the testimony of witnesses or during the attorney's statements to the jury at the beginning and end of trial. For all intents and purposes, the evidence would be treated as if it did not exist. In order for the government to convict the defendant of a federal crime, the government would be required to produce other evidence that was obtained without violating the defendant's constitutional rights.

The *Weeks* decision made it clear that if a federal trial court allowed the jury to see or hear about illegally seized evidence during a defendant's trial, and if the defendant were convicted, that is, if he or she were found guilty of the crime, the defendant's criminal conviction should be reversed by a higher court on appeal. The procedure for appealing a criminal conviction is basically the same as it was during the *Weeks* era.

Generally, if a defendant believes the trial court erred in allowing certain evidence at trial, the defendant can ask a higher court, sometimes called a court of appeals, to review his or her case. If the court of appeals agrees with the defendant, it will reverse the defendant's conviction. It will strike the defendant's conviction from the record, and order the trial court to conduct a new trial without the use of the improper evidence. If the court of appeals disagrees with the defendant in a state case, the defendant can appeal to a state court of last resort, usually called a state supreme court. If it is a federal case where the defendant was convicted in a federal district court and circuit court of appeals, the defendant can then appeal directly to the United States Supreme Court.

A defendant seeking review of conviction by the Supreme Court is first required to file a legal document called a *Petition for Writ of Certiorari. Certiorari*, a Latin term, means "to be made certain."[15] A *Petition for Writ of Certiorari* calls "for delivery to a higher court of the record of a proceeding before a lower court."[16] The document generally describes the legal issues that the defendant, now called the petitioner, wants the higher court to review. The government can file a brief in opposition, urging the Court not to grant the petition. If the Supreme Court determines that the legal issues require review by the highest level court in the country's judicial system—for example, if they are new issues that have not yet been decided by the Court or if there is a conflict among appellate courts around the country as to how the issue should be resolved—the Supreme Court will agree to hear the case and grant the petition.

The petitioner must then submit a brief thoroughly explaining the issues and the law supporting the theory. The government will have an opportunity to respond to the petitioner's brief. Sometimes another person or group, known as an *amicus curiae*, or "friend of the court," will volunteer or be invited by the Court to file a separate brief giving advice to the Court on the pending matter.[17] After the Court has reviewed all the briefs, it will hear oral argument from the attorneys representing each of the parties. Then it will consider the issues and render a decision.

Mr. Weeks appealed his case all the way to the United States Supreme Court. There it was decided that the trial court had improperly admitted evidence against him at his trial. Therefore, the Supreme Court reversed his conviction and ordered a new trial. Remember, though, that Mr. Weeks's case was a federal case and at the time the reach of the Fourth Amendment was limited to federal courts.

The *Weeks* decision established a precedent, an example, that would begin a long and intense debate among future Supreme Court Justices as to the proper remedy for violations of the Fourth and Fifth Amendments. More crucial to Dolly Mapp's case was whether that remedy would ever be applied to state court criminal cases. An important part of the debate centered on the many different reactions state courts had to the *Weeks* decision in the years to come.

When the United States Supreme Court renders a decision instructing state courts to apply a particular law in a particular way, state courts must comply. But in *Weeks*, the United States Supreme Court declined to apply the Fourth and Fifth Amendments in state criminal cases. Where did that leave the state courts? It allowed each state to develop its own law as to whether evidence seized in violation of a defendant's constitutional rights would be admissible in the courts in that particular state.

As of 1948, thirty-one states rejected the "exclusionary rule" announced in *Weeks*.[18] Those thirty-one states decided that even if evidence had been seized illegally, according to federal standards, it would still be admissible against a defendant in a state criminal trial. One of those thirty-one states was Ohio, Mapp's home state. Only sixteen states agreed with the *Weeks* decision as of 1948, and those states excluded illegally seized evidence from their state criminal trials.[19]

These contrary views formed the backdrop for the 1948 Supreme Court decision in *Wolf* v. *Colorado*. In *Wolf*, a deputy sheriff entered Dr. Julius A. Wolf's office without a warrant and seized his appointment book. The sheriff searched through the book to find the names and addresses of Dr. Wolf's patients, then contacted and interrogated some of them. The seized book was used in evidence against Dr. Wolf in a state criminal court, and Dr. Wolf was convicted of conspiracy to commit abortion. Abortion was not legal in this country at that time.

Up until then, the Supreme Court had clearly drawn the line. The limitations of the Fourth Amendment right to privacy applied only to federal cases. If Wolf's case had been brought to federal court, the illegally seized evidence would not have been admissible. But Dr. Wolf was prosecuted in a state court.

United States Supreme Court Justice Felix Frankfurter wrote the opinion for the *Wolf* Court.

Unlike the *Weeks* Court, Justice Frankfurter did not focus only on the Fourth Amendment. He referred to another constitutional amendment—the Fourteenth Amendment. In doing so, he took a giant step that would eventually affect Dolly Mapp's case.

The Fourteenth Amendment to the Constitution, adopted in 1868, prohibits any state from depriving any person ". . . of life, liberty, or property, without due process of law . . ."[20] This is known as the "due process clause" of the Fourteenth Amendment. Due process means that before the state can take away a person's life, freedom, or property, that person is entitled to a fair hearing that must follow certain standard rules of procedure. How did the Fourteenth Amendment relate to the Fourth Amendment?

To Justice Frankfurter, the Fourth Amendment's guarantee of privacy is of basic, fundamental importance to our society.[21] Even though the Fourteenth Amendment does not specifically mention unreasonable searches and seizures, Justice Frankfurter wrote that the Fourth Amendment right of privacy is implied in the Fourteenth Amendment's concept of liberty. Therefore, he reasoned, the due process clause of the Fourteenth Amendment requires the states to enforce the Fourth Amendment's guarantee of privacy. In other words, the Supreme Court determined that the

Justice Felix Frankfurter wrote the opinion for the Court in the 1948 case of *Wolf* v. *Colorado*. In this case the Supreme Court had to examine the validity of the Fourth Amendment when applied to individual states.

Fourteenth Amendment incorporated the fundamental rights of the Fourth Amendment.

Now that the United States Supreme Court recognized that the principles set forth in the Fourth Amendment were part of the Fourteenth Amendment's due process clause, would it carry that reasoning to the next step? Would it rule, as it had done in federal cases, that illegally seized evidence is inadmissible in a state criminal proceeding?

It would not do so in the *Wolf* case. The Supreme Court held that even though the Fourth Amendment placed certain restrictions on *federal* courts, the Fourteenth Amendment did not place those same restrictions on *state* courts. The question was not whether a state violated a defendant's constitutional rights when state law enforcement officers seized evidence without a valid search warrant. That, Justice Frankfurter wrote, would certainly violate the Fourteenth Amendment. The real question was: What remedy is appropriate if a state violates the Fourteenth Amendment?

Justice Frankfurter noted that the *Weeks* exclusionary rule did not come directly from the Fourth Amendment because there is nothing in the Fourth Amendment that specifically calls for excluding illegally seized evidence. According to Justice Frankfurter, the exclusionary rule was a rule of "judicial implication," meaning that the Supreme Court designed the rule on its own as a way to remedy a violation of the Fourth Amendment. The *Wolf* Court was unwilling, however, to apply the same rule to a violation of the Fourteenth Amendment, even though the Fourteenth Amendment contained the same guarantees as the Fourth Amendment. Why not?

The Court considered that in the thirty-one states where there was still no exclusionary rule, other remedies were available to a person whose constitutional right to privacy was violated. Some states, for example, allowed civil lawsuits for monetary damages against the searching law enforcement officers; other states provided for criminal sanctions against an officer who obtained a warrant he or she knew was invalid.[22] The *Wolf* court valued the states' experience in determining the most appropriate remedy for their individual communities. Even though exclusion of the evidence may have prevented unreasonable searches and seizures, the *Wolf* court felt that other remedies that the states had made available were just as effective.

Another debate was emerging, too. Whom would the exclusionary rule really protect? Justice Frankfurter recognized that exclusion of illegally seized evidence primarily served the individual on whose person or property incriminating evidence was found—the criminal defendant. But what about society's need to prevent crime? Each state and the Supreme Court struggled to strike some balance between these two interests.

Justices Douglas and Murphy did not agree with the Supreme Court's refusal to apply the exclusionary rule in Dr. Wolf's case. But they were in the minority. Because the Supreme Court uses a democratic system just like our electoral college voting system, the majority rules. Whatever outcome the majority of Justices agree on becomes the law of the land.

Those Justices who do not agree with the majority may still write separate opinions expressing their own views about how the case should be decided. Those opinions are called "dissenting opinions." Although dissenting opinions are not the law of the court, they often provide unique insight into how a particular case was decided and how future cases may be decided.

The dissenting opinions of Justice Douglas and Justice Murphy expressed their dismay with the majority's decision. Even though the majority found that the Fourteenth Amendment prohibits the same activities prohibited by the Fourth Amendment, it would not take the next step and apply the exclusionary rule to state criminal courts. Their objections would continue to fuel this debate for the next eleven years. During this time, the Supreme Court continued to review petitions from criminal defendants who described various instances of police abuse in seizing evidence. The decisions that the Supreme Court handed down after the *Wolf* case show how difficult it was becoming to define an appropriate remedy that could be used in all cases.

In *Rochin* v. *California*, a state case, the police directed a doctor to forcibly use a stomach pump to extract evidence of illegal drug use from Antonio Rochin's stomach.[23] The Supreme Court was outraged. But despite the Court's heavy reliance on the concepts of search and seizure law and self-incrimination in other important cases, it did not rely at all on those concepts when it reversed Rochin's conviction. It formed an entirely new rule—that because the police conduct was so offensive to our standards of decency and fairness, the conduct violated the due process clause of the Fourteenth Amendment.

Would "brutal and offensive police conduct" become the new test for whether evidence should be excluded? Apparently not.

In 1954, the Supreme Court heard the case of *Irvine* v. *California*.[24] In that state case, police officers made a key to Patrick Irvine's home and without a search warrant, they entered his house on three different occasions. They installed concealed microphones so that they could listen, by eavesdropping—rather than by wiretapping from outside—to the defendant's conversations. They suspected that he was involved in illegal gambling operations. The police officers testified at Irvine's trial about the conversations that they overheard, and Irvine was convicted.

Justice Frankfurter wanted the Court to exclude the evidence as it had done in *Rochin* v. *California* because he felt that the police conduct was "repulsive."[25] Justice Douglas wanted to exclude the evidence, but on the grounds that the police conduct violated the Fourth Amendment right of privacy. Justice Black believed there was a violation of the defendant's Fifth Amendment right against self-incrimination. He, too, wanted the Court to exclude the evidence.

The majority of the Justices disagreed with those proposals. Justice Robert H. Jackson, who wrote the opinion for the Court, focused again on how the individual states were dealing with the problem of unlawfully seized evidence. He pointed out that until that time, there had been no reliable evidence that the states that excluded illegally seized evidence had fewer illegal searches and seizures than those states that admitted illegally seized evidence.

The majority of the Justices also had the same concern addressed by the *Wolf* Court. They believed that even if the evidence were seized unlawfully, excluding the evidence at trial would result in protecting only the criminals. It would do nothing, however, to protect innocent persons from illegal searches where the police did not find any evidence of a crime. Interestingly, Justice Frankfurter had opposed excluding unlawfully seized evidence in the *Wolf* case for the same reasons. But he now wanted the Court to exclude the unlawfully seized evidence in the *Irvine* case.

After considerable debate among the Justices, the *Irvine* Court affirmed, or upheld, the defendant's conviction, again refusing to require state courts to exclude illegally seized evidence from state criminal trials. That decision was handed down three years before the police raided Dolly Mapp's home in Ohio.

In June 1960, the Supreme Court had another opportunity to decide whether to extend the federal exclusionary rule to the states. This time the case involved a slightly new twist. The issue was whether evidence illegally seized by state law enforcement officers could be admitted during trial in a *federal* court.

In *Elkins* v. *United States*, Oregon state law enforcement officers used a search warrant to seize evidence against the defendants, whom they suspected of possessing obscene pictures.[26] The officers did not find any obscene materials but they did discover evidence that the defendants had been illegally tapping into telephone lines. A closer review of the search warrant by the Oregon trial court showed that it was not valid; therefore, the trial court dismissed the case against the defendants.

That was not the end of the case, however. Based on the evidence the Oregon officers discovered, the defendants were later charged with violating a federal telephone communications law. During their trial in federal court, the judge permitted the prosecutor to admit the evidence that was seized by the Oregon state law enforcement officers.

Like the *Wolf* and the *Irvine* courts had done before, the *Elkins* Court again noticed the pulse of the country. It wanted to know where each state stood on the issue of whether evidence illegally seized was admissible in a state court. It found that in twenty-six states, evidence illegally seized by state law enforcement officers was inadmissible at trial in a state court.[27] Twenty-four states still admitted such evidence.[28] Significantly, of those that excluded the evidence, several excluded not only evidence seized by *state* law enforcement officers, but also evidence unlawfully seized by *federal* officers.

That information was very important to the *Elkins* Court for it was concerned about a number of issues. Courts and communities around the country were still grappling with the pros and cons of an exclusionary rule. Those against the exclusionary rule believed it meant that criminals would go free merely because a police officer had blundered. Those in favor of the rule felt it was necessary to deter unlawful conduct by the police and to compel respect for the Constitution. The intensity of the debate came to light every time a convicted defendant petitioned the Supreme Court for review of the issue.

The *Elkins* Court was also concerned with avoiding needless conflict between state and federal courts. Until that time, the exclusionary rule was clear cut. Evidence unlawfully seized by federal agents was inadmissible in a federal court (*Weeks*). Whether evidence unlawfully seized by state agents was admissible in a state court was left to the individual states to decide (*Wolf*), except where the police conduct was particularly outrageous (*Rochin*). Under no circumstances did either a federal or state exlusionary rule apply to searches conducted by private detectives or private citizens (*Burdeau* v. *McDowell*).[29]

What problems would arise if a federal court located in a state that has an exclusionary rule for its own state courts admitted evidence unlawfully seized by a state officer? If the case had been brought in state court the evidence would not be admitted. The *Elkins* Court predicted that it may lead to less cooperation between state and federal law enforcement officers. That problem would not occur if all law enforcement officers knew that evidence unlawfully seized by either state or federal officers would not be used in federal court.

Despite the concerns of the *Wolf* and *Irvine* Courts that excluding unlawfully seized evidence would mean that criminals would go free, the *Elkins* Court took the opposite approach. Ruling that evidence obtained unlawfully by *state* law enforcement officers is inadmissible in a *federal* criminal trial, the Court relied on the writings of former Justice Brandeis more than thirty years before:

> Crime is contagious. If the Government becomes a lawbreaker, it breeds contempt for law; it invites every man to become a law unto himself; it invites anarchy. To declare that in the administration of the criminal law the end justifies the means—to declare that the Government may commit crimes in order to secure the conviction of a private criminal—would bring terrible retribution.[30]

The stage was set for Dolly Mapp's case, which the Supreme Court would hear less than nine months after it decided the *Elkins* case. Clearly, it had been heading toward a ruling that would require the states to exclude unlawfully seized evidence from state trials, but would it? It was time for Mapp's lawyers to try to persuade the Court to take that final step.

3

Mapp States Her Case

Dolly Mapp's problems arose during an era when American society had little tolerance for pornography. In 1957, the year Mapp was arrested, it was a felony crime under Section 2905.34 of the Ohio Revised Code for any person to "knowingly have in his possession or under his control an obscene, lewd or lascivious book, magazine, pamphlet, paper, writing, advertisement, circular, print, picture, photograph, or pictures and stories of immoral deeds, lust or crime." A felony is a serious crime punishable by at least one year in prison. Ohio lawmakers in the state legislature had made possession of obscene materials punishable by not less than one year and not more than seven years in prison.

After her arrest on May 23, 1957, Dolly Mapp first had to contend with the misdemeanor charge of possession of gambling paraphernalia, a less serious charge under Ohio law. Her case was tried in police court and the judge found her not guilty. It was not until after her trial in police court that she was formally charged with the more serious charge of possession of obscene materials, a felony.

Unlike the misdemeanor charge, it took more than Mapp's arrest on the felony charge to proceed to trial. First the prosecutor had to present evidence about the case to a grand jury and obtain an indictment.

A grand jury is a group of citizens who are summoned together by the government to hear the testimony of witnesses and examine evidence in a closed room in order to determine whether a suspect should be charged with a particular crime. The grand jurors must decide two things based on the evidence presented to them: (1) whether there is probable cause to believe that a crime has been committed, and (2) whether it is more likely than not that the suspect is the person who committed the crime. If it decides the suspect should be prosecuted, the grand jury will formally charge the suspect in a document called an indictment.

A grand jury should not be confused with a petit jury. Unlike petit jurors, grand jurors do not decide if a suspect is guilty or not guilty. They only decide if there is enough evidence to proceed with the case. Petit jurors, on the other hand, actually hear the trial in the courtroom and decide the case. Unlike the proceedings in a trial courtroom, the only persons allowed in the grand jury room are the grand jurors, the prosecutor, and the witness who is testifying. There is no judge, defense attorney, or defendant. Also, all grand jury deliberations are secret, whereas trial court proceedings, with very few exceptions, are open to the public.

Almost four months after Dolly Mapp was arrested, a grand jury formally charged her with knowingly possessing certain lewd books, pictures, and photographs.[1] Her case was now ready to proceed through the criminal justice process.

In every criminal case, the defendant must either plead guilty, not guilty, or *nolo contendere*, a Latin phrase that means "I do not wish to contest." If a defendant admits guilt, generally the next step will be for the court, meaning the judge hearing the case, to impose sentence and close the case. If the defendant denies guilt, the case will proceed to trial. By pleading *nolo contendere* a defendant neither admits nor denies the charges. This special plea has the effect of a guilty plea, however, and permits the judge to sentence the defendant just as though a guilty plea had been made. During the fifteen months following Dolly Mapp's arrest, she initially pleaded guilty, then later withdrew

INDICTMENT FOR   POSSESSION OBSCENE LITERATURE   R C 2905.34

The State of Ohio. ss.
CUYAHOGA COUNTY

Of the term of........................ SEPTEMBER

In the year of our Lord one thousand nine hundred and .... FIFTY SEVEN

The Jurors of the Grand Jury of the State of Ohio, within and for the body of the County afore-

said, on their oaths, IN THE NAME AND BY THE AUTHORITY OF THE STATE OF OHIO.

Do Find and Present. That.............. Dolly Mapp   (Dollree Mapp)

on or about the .....23rd..... day of .... May .... 19 57 . , at the County aforesaid,

unlawfully and knowingly had in her possession and under her
control, certain lewd and lascivious Books, Pictures and
Photographs, said Books, Pictures and Photographs being
so indecent and immoral in their nature that the same
would be offensive to the Court and improper to be placed
upon the records thereof

68326

00565

contrary to the form of the statute in such case made and provided, and against the peace and dignity
of the State of Ohio.

John T Corrigan
Prosecuting Attorney.

The grand jury formally charged, or indicted, Dolly Mapp on charges of knowingly possessing certain lewd books, pictures, and photographs. Her case could now proceed through the criminal justice system.

her guilty plea, and pleaded not guilty. She then demanded a trial by jury.

Dolly Mapp's trial began in the Cuyahoga County Court of Common Pleas in Cleveland, Ohio, on September 3, 1958. She was represented by Alexander L. Kearns, a sixty-two-year-old attorney who had been practicing law in Ohio for forty-two years.[2] He was associated with Walter L. Greene, a thirty-three-year-old attorney who had been practicing law for only five years. Greene was the attorney who was waiting outside Dolly Mapp's house during the police search.

Just before trial, Kearns filed a motion asking the court to prevent the jurors from hearing about or seeing any of the evidence the police had seized from Mapp's home. Kearns's request is called a motion to suppress evidence. Kearns argued that because the police did not have a search warrant particularly naming the obscene materials mentioned in the indictment, the search for and seizure of those items violated Ohio state law; therefore, the government should not be permitted to introduce them as evidence at trial.

Kearns had an uphill battle though. At the time of his motion, Ohio followed a 1936 rule of law set forth in the case of *State* v. *Lindway*.[3] In *Lindway*, evidence was unlawfully seized from the home of Mike J. Lindway, who had been suspected of bombing the

In the months following Dolly Mapp's arrest, she initially pleaded guilty to the charges against her. She later withdrew the guilty plea, pleaded not guilty, and demanded a trial by jury.

homes of employees of a manufacturing company where he had formerly worked. The Supreme Court of Ohio upheld Lindway's conviction and ruled that illegally seized evidence was admissible in an Ohio state criminal trial because the Fourth Amendment did not apply to the states. Ohio had a different remedy for unlawful police action—the defendant could sue the police for trespass.

Following the *Lindway* rule, Judge Donald F. Lybarger rejected Kearns's argument and overruled his motion to suppress the evidence seized from Dolly Mapp's home.

When the trial began, the prosecutor called only two witnesses against Dolly Mapp—Officer Michael Haney and Sergeant Carl Delau—two of the police officers who searched Mapp's home. Attorney Walter L. Greene and Dolores Clark, a friend of Mapp's, testified for the defense. Dolly Mapp also took the stand in her own defense.

Under our system of justice, the prosecution has the burden of proving beyond a reasonable doubt each element of the offense that the defendant is charged with committing. For example, most criminal laws require that the prosecutor prove not only that the defendant committed the criminal act but also that he or she did so knowingly and intentionally. In Dolly Mapp's case,

STATE OF OHIO   )   IN THE COURT OF COMMON PLEAS
)   CASE NO. 68326
COUNTY OF CUYAHOGA) SS.

STATE OF OHIO   )
         Plaintiff)
)
    vs.   )
)
DOLLY MAPP   )
        Defendant)

68326
MOTION TO SUPPRESS
EVIDENCE

00570 **36091**

    Now comes the defendant by her attorney, A. L. Kearns
and moves this honorable court for an order suppressing the
evidence procured by the police officers, to wit:

    Certain claimed lewd and lascivious Books, Pictures and
Photographs and intended to be used in evidence in the trial
of the aforesaid cause.

    For the reason that the aforesaid evidence was not pro-
cured by a proper search warrant as ~~provided~~ submitted by Section
2905.35 of the Ohio Revised Code.

                          A. L. Kearns
                    Attorney for Defendant

           NOTICE

    The State of Ohio will take notice that the defendant has
filed the aforesaid motion and that the same will be set for
hearing in Court Room No. 1 of the Court of Common Pleas Criminal Branch in accordance with the rules of said court.

LAW OFFICES
KEARNS, GREENE & GREENE
1101 HIPPODROME BUILDING
CLEVELAND 14, OHIO

                           A. L. Kearns
                    Attorney for Defendant

                                      2

        6. That the court erred in over-ruling the
motion of the defendant for a directed verdict of discharge
upon the resting by the state of Ohio.

        7. That the court erred in over-ruling the
motion for a directed verdict at the close of all of the evidence.

        8. Other errors appearing on the face of the
record and duly objected to by the defense.

                          A. L. Kearns
            A. L. KEARNS
            Attorney for the Defendant
            1101 Hippodrome Bldg.
            Cleveland 14, Ohio
            MAin 1-3543

                00573

               68326

A copy of the Motion to Suppress Evidence, filed by Dolly Mapp's attorney
in the Court of Common Pleas, is shown here. Mapp's attorney argued
that since police had never actually presented a search warrant, the search
they conducted was illegal, making any evidence they found inadmissible
in court.

the prosecutor had the burden of proving that Mapp knew the obscene literature was inside her house and that she intentionally had possession and control of those items.

Sergeant Delau and Officer Haney testified that they found the obscene materials, including pencil sketches and four books entitled *London Stage Affairs, Affairs of a Troubadour, Memoirs of a Hotel Man,* and *Little Darlings,* inside the drawers of Mapp's bedroom bureaus and inside her suitcase, which was also in the bedroom.[4] If the jury believed that the police officers found the items inside Mapp's bedroom as the police officer testified, that was enough to prove that Dolly Mapp possessed the items according to Ohio law. Mapp contradicted the officers' testimony though. She told the jury that the officers could only have found those items inside a box in the basement because that was where she and her friend Dolores Clark had put them. In fact, she testified that while she was sitting handcuffed in the bedroom Officer Haney walked into the room holding a brown paper bag containing the obscene materials she had packed away in the basement.

She also told the jury all about Morris Jones, the man who she insisted was the owner of the obscene material. She explained that he had rented a room in her home on and off for about a year. After he left for

Policy House Closed After 3-Hour Siege

Police Break In, Arrest Former Mrs. Bivins

By JERRY BALLINGER

The "California Gold" policy house abruptly went out of business yesterday after a three-hour police siege of the home of Miss Dollree Mapp.

She is the former wife of Boxer Jimmy Bivins and the former girl friend of Light Heavyweight Champion Archie Moore.

Miss Mapp, 29, of 14705 Milverton Road S. E. (or 4786 Lee Road S. E., depending on where she is staying), was jailed. She and Virgil Ogletree, 34, of 1355 E. 115th Street, were nabbed at the Milverton address.

Sgt. Carl J. Delau and Patrolmen Thomas J. Dever and Michael J. Haney, members of Lt. Martin L. Cooney's special investigating unit, led the raid —but before it was over they needed help from Four District policemen.

And they needed a search warrant. Miss Mapp was, they said, stubborn about letting them inside.

Receives Tip

The raid came, Cooney said, after he had received a tip that a man who knew something about the Monday bombing of the home of numbers operator Donald (The Kid) Young was staying at the Milverton address. The informant also told Cooney that Miss Mapp's home was being used as a policy house.

This, it turned out, was the "California Gold" policy house. The officers seized a large trunk full of slips and records and other policy paraphernalia. They also discovered a quantity of books, pamphlets and photgraphs they described as "obscene."

Ogletree, identified as the owner of the Friendly Service Dry Cleaners, 2365 E. 55th (Continued on Page 11, Column 4)

"California Gold" Strike

Sgt. Carl J. Delau examines a trunkful of policy slips found in the home of Miss Dollree Mapp, ex-wife of boxer Jimmy Bivins and former girl friend of Archie Moore, light heavyweight champion of the world.

Policy House Closed After 3-Hour Siege

★ **From First Page**

Street, is involved in policy here, Delau said. Both Miss Mapp and Ogletree were undergoing extensive questioning last night in connection with the bombing.

How It Went

Delau gave this description of the raid:

Delau, Dever and Haney banged on the door and demanded admittance.

Miss Mapp, who was in the upstairs half of the double house, leaned out a window and asked them what they wanted. They told her.

"No!" she shouted down to them. "I won't let you in! Go away! You can't come in without a search warrant!"

Delau told her that could be arranged.

Thus the seige began.

Reinforcements arrived from the Fourth District. The warrant arrived from Central Police Station. Again Delau demanded that Miss Mapp let them in. Again Miss Mapp refused.

This time, armed with the warrant plus some brawn, the officers pried open a screen door, broke the glass on an inner door and entered Miss Mapp's home. They found the trunk, opened it, saw what was inside.

But not without one desperate last-ditch act of defiance from Miss Mapp. She met the policemen on the stairs. She grabbed the warrant from the hand of one of them.

Then she stuffed it down the front of her dress.

The raiders were startled, to say the least. But one of them

rolled up a sleeve and said to her: "If you don't get it for us, I will."

She returned the warrant.

Ogletree, who had sneaked down the back stairs, was found in the downstairs home. A woman who lived there said he had threatened her.

Miss Mapp gave her home address as the one on Lee Road. Her lawyer, Walter L. Greene, was on hand at the final stages of the seige. She had phoned him. He followed the police entourage downtown.

Miss Mapp has a daughter, Barbara Bivins, 13. The girl was not at home at the time of the raid.

Miss Mapp, who also calls herself Dolly Mapp, has been on the outs with Moore for some time. They have been involved in various suits against each other.

Sergeant Carl Delau (shown here looking into a trunk full of gambling slips) and Officer Michael Haney were two of the police officers who conducted an extensive search of Dolly Mapp's home.

vacation in New York earlier in 1957, Mapp learned from his mother that he would not be returning to Ohio. She decided to pack up his belongings and store them until he or his mother could pick them up.

The pencil sketches were the only obscene items belonging to Jones that Mapp admitted were inside her bedroom. She had stored the sketches, she testified, inside her suitcase along with Jones's gun and some of his other belongings. Mapp's longtime friend, Dolores Clark, corroborated—confirmed or verified—Mapp's account because she was the one who had helped Mapp pack up Jones's belongings.

It is quite common for witnesses who testify at a trial to give different versions of what happened. This does not necessarily mean that one person is telling the truth and the other is lying, although that may be the case. Inconsistent or differing testimony may also occur because people often see or recall things in different ways. It was not unusual, then, that the witnesses called to testify in Dolly Mapp's case gave several different versions of what happened on May 23, 1957.

The trial testimony most crucial to the future of Dolly Mapp's case had nothing to do with what evidence was seized or where it was seized, however. Rather, it concerned the conduct of the police officers and the search warrant. Officer Haney, one of the first officers to arrive at Mapp's house, testified that Mapp voluntarily let the officers into her home on May 23. But Sergeant Delau confirmed Greene's and Mapp's testimony that the officers pried open a door and forced their way in.

The evidence concerning the search warrant was downright mysterious. Officer Haney and Sergeant Delau testified that the police had a search warrant when they entered Dolly Mapp's home. Mapp, however, described her ordeal like this:

> When they came in I said, "Inspector, I want to see the search warrant." And I was standing on the top landing of the stairs, and I didn't know who the inspector was when he was in plain clothes. He said, "Here is the search warrant." He held it back from me, and I remember Mr. Greene told me I should see it and read it, and I told him I wanted to see it. He said "You can't see it." At that I reached over, took the search warrant from his hand and put it down in my bosom . . . [O]ne of them said "What are we going to do now?" The one that grabbed me said "I'm going down after it." I said, "No, you are not." He went down anyway.[5]

Did the police officers really have a search warrant? Neither officer had brought the warrant to court. Neither officer knew where it was or could say what it stated. In fact, the prosecutor did not call *any* witnesses who could tell the jury what was in the search warrant. Even more intriguing, the prosecutor did not produce the warrant for the court or the jury to read at any time during the trial.

Remember, though, that the judge had already ruled that the evidence the police seized could be admitted at trial even if the police did not have a valid search warrant. The jury never had to consider the absence of a search warrant—the judge had already decided that issue as a matter of law. That meant that the jury was required to concern itself only with the factual evidence admitted and whether that evidence proved beyond a reasonable doubt that Dolly Mapp knowingly possessed obscene literature.

At the end of the trial the jurors deliberated; they discussed the case among themselves and found Mapp guilty of possessing obscene materials. The fact that the government did not produce a search warrant had no effect on the outcome of Mapp's trial, but several years later it would ultimately be of great importance to the United States Supreme Court and to all other state courts around the country.

Judge Lybarger sentenced Dolly Mapp to imprisonment in the Ohio Reformatory for Women for not less than one and not more than seven years. The court agreed to postpone her sentence until after she appealed her case but required her to post a bond of twenty-five hundred dollars. A friend posted the bond for her.[6]

Mapp's lawyers, Kearns and Greene, then began the long road through the appellate court process.

Their first appeal to the Eighth District Court of Appeals of Ohio claimed that the trial court had made nine errors and, therefore, Mapp's conviction should be reversed. One claim that would become a central issue in later appeals challenged the constitutionality of Ohio's obscenity statute. Dolly Mapp's lawyers argued that the statute was overly broad because it punished persons like Mapp merely for storing material that belonged to someone else. Kearns also challenged the

This is a copy of the jury verdict that was rendered September 4, 1958. It shows that Dolly Mapp was found guilty on the charge of possession of obscene literature.

search of Mapp's house without a valid search warrant. The Court of Appeals did not agree that the trial court had made a mistake and it affirmed, or upheld, Dolly Mapp's conviction.

The next appeal was to the Supreme Court of Ohio, the highest court in that state. Again Mapp's attorneys argued, among many other issues, that the Ohio obscenity statute was unconstitutional and that the obscene literature should not have been admitted into evidence at her trial because it was seized during an unlawful search. Interestingly, four Justices voted that the obscenity statute was unconstitutional. Those Justices felt that Mapp's conviction should be reversed. However, before the Ohio Supreme Court could declare a law unconstitutional, the Ohio Constitution required that six of the seven Justices agree. Because only four of the seven Justices found the obscenity statute unconstitutional, the Ohio Supreme Court could not nullify it.

The Supreme Court of Ohio also agreed with the Court of Appeals about the search warrant issue, and it also affirmed Dolly Mapp's conviction. Justice Taft's written opinion, however, would ultimately be of great interest to the United States Supreme Court. In that opinion, Justice Taft noted that in the trial record there was "considerable doubt as to whether there ever was any warrant for the search of defendant's home. No warrant was offered in evidence, there was no testimony as to who issued any warrant or as to what any warrant contained, and the absence from evidence of any such warrant is not explained or otherwise accounted for in the record."[7]

Nevertheless, the court relied upon its earlier decision in *State* v. *Lindway*, which held that evidence obtained by an unlawful search and seizure is admissible in a criminal trial in the state of Ohio. Even though the lack of a search warrant appeared to bother the court, it refused to change the law in Ohio as other courts had done in some states after the United States Supreme Court decision in *Wolf* v. *Colorado*.

After this second appellate defeat, Dolly Mapp and her attorneys had one last appeal available—an appeal to the United States Supreme Court. It was going to be very expensive though, and Mapp did not have the money, nearly eight thousand dollars.[8] Fortunately, a friend helped her again.

Dolly Mapp's attorneys filed a notice of appeal to the United States Supreme Court on June 15, 1960. It had taken more than three years from the day the police raided her home to reach the highest court in the country. Mapp's case also gained the attention of the American Civil Liberties Union (ACLU). ACLU attorney Bernard

Berkman of the Ohio office agreed to file an *amicus curiae*, friend-of-the-court brief, on Mapp's behalf.

Interestingly, the search and seizure issue that would ultimately change the course of legal history was only fleetingly addressed in Dolly Mapp's brief to the Supreme Court. It consumed only *three sentences* of the ACLU's brief. Although both briefs argued that the unlawful search violated Mapp's constitutional rights and, therefore, that the evidence should not have been admitted, the arguments only touched the tip of the iceberg.

Alexander Kearns and Walter Greene cited only two cases to support their claim that the unlawful search violated Dolly Mapp's rights under the Fourth, Fifth, and Fourteenth Amendments of the United States Constitution, and under Article 1 of the Ohio Constitution. They wrote that the conduct of the police on May 23, 1957, "portrays a shocking disregard of human rights," similar to *Rochin* v. *California.* In this case the Court reversed Antonio Rochin's conviction because the police had pumped his stomach to get evidence of drug use.[9] Dolly Mapp's attorneys also found some support in Ohio State Supreme Court Justice Herbert's dissenting opinion in Dolly Mapp's case.

Justice Herbert wanted the Ohio Supreme Court to modify the *Lindway* rule because there was no evidence at trial that Dolly Mapp intended to distribute or circulate the obscene material found inside her home. It was Justice Herbert's opinion that private possession of obscene literature should not be a crime if there is no distribution. If, as Justice Herbert contended, Dolly Mapp was not a criminal, then she should have been protected from the unlawful search and seizure. The way to protect her, Justice Herbert wrote, was to exclude the evidence the police seized unlawfully. Justice Herbert was very concerned that the broad scope of the *Lindway* rule could lead to police abuse and violations of constitutional rights.

Similar to Mapp's brief, the main thrust of the ACLU brief addressed the constitutionality of the Ohio obscenity statute. It devoted only three sentences to the search and seizure issue, claiming that the unlawful search violated the due process clause of the Fourteenth Amendment. In one sentence the ACLU asked the court to re-examine *Wolf* v. *Colorado* and "conclude that the ordered liberty concept guaranteed to persons by the due process clause of the Fourteenth Amendment necessarily requires that evidence illegally obtained in violation thereof, not be admissible in state criminal proceedings."[10] Their briefs filed, Mapp, her attorneys, and the ACLU waited for the government's response. How would the government address the issues they had raised?

4

The State of Ohio Responds

At the time of Dolly Mapp's arrest, Gertrude Bauer Mahon had been practicing law in Ohio for sixteen years. Born in 1904, she attended Mary Manse College in Toledo, Ohio, and then continued her education at John Marshall Law School, now known as Cleveland Marshall Law School.[1] She was one of only a few women who graduated from law school during the early 1940s.

In the summer of 1957, Mahon worked as an assistant prosecutor in the office of the Cuyahoga County prosecutor, John T. Corrigan. She was assigned the responsibility of prosecuting, or seeking legal punishment for, Dolly Mapp for possessing obscene materials. It was an assignment that would ultimately lead to her appearance before the esteemed Justices of the United States Supreme Court to present and argue the State of Ohio's case.

A county prosecuting attorney represents the interests of the state in all criminal cases filed in that county. For crimes where there is an actual victim—for instance, in a robbery, theft, rape, or homicide case—the victim is the complainant and the prosecutor files charges against a suspect and prosecutes the case on behalf of the state. In essence, the prosecutor is the victim's attorney.

Who was the victim in Dolly Mapp's case? Some people believe that crimes such as gambling, prostitution, and illegal possession of drugs or obscene materials are victimless crimes, meaning that no one is a victim and, therefore, that persons who commit those acts should not be prosecuted. Others believe, however, that all of the citizens of a state are victims when someone violates the laws of that state. The victims that Assistant Prosecutor Mahon sought to protect against Dolly Mapp's crime were the citizens of the State of Ohio.

Mahon won a key legal victory shortly before the trial began. Judge Lybarger overruled Mapp's attorney's motion to suppress the evidence. In most cases the prosecutor responds in writing to any motions filed by the defense attorney. Mahon did not even respond to Mapp's attorney's motion, however, because at that time the *Lindway* case clearly expressed the law in Ohio—evidence was admissible at trial even if it was unlawfully seized. Judge Lybarger's ruling meant that Mahon could introduce the obscene materials taken from Dolly Mapp's home as evidence against her even if the police did not have a search warrant.

Under our criminal justice system, the defendant is always presumed innocent until proven guilty. The government has the burden of proof in a criminal case. That means that the prosecutor, as the state or federal government's attorney, must prove to the jury that the defendant is guilty beyond a reasonable doubt. It is not up to the defendant to prove innocence. In Mapp's case, Mahon had to prove to the jury that Dolly Mapp knowingly possessed obscene materials on May 23, 1957. Mahon decided that she could prove her case by calling two police witnesses to the stand.

Because Judge Lybarger had already resolved the search warrant issue, it was unnecessary for Mahon to question the police officers about how they entered Mapp's house. Nevertheless, Mahon did ask those questions during her direct examination. Her presentation of the case established crucial facts on which the United States Supreme Court would later rely.

Under our criminal justice system, Dolly Mapp, as the defendant, was presumed innocent until proven guilty. The government had to prove her guilt in a court of law. In an attempt to do this, the lawyer for the state of Ohio questioned two of the police officers involved in the arrest. One of the arresting officers, Carl Delau, is shown here.

Mahon asked Officer Haney to describe what happened when he arrived at Mapp's home. He responded, "A search warrant was brought out after an hour and a half or two-hour delay, brought to the premises, and the officers were admitted by Mrs. Mapp from the sidewalk."[2] That response opened the door for cross-examination by Kearns, Mapp's attorney, on the issue of the search warrant. The following exchange occurred between Kearns and Officer Haney:

Q. Where is that search warrant?

A. I don't know.

Q. Do you have it here?

A. I don't have it.

Q. Would you tell the jury who has it?

A. I can't tell the jury who has it; no sir.

Q. And you were one of the investigating officers in the investigation by the police department?

A. Yes.

Q. But you can't tell us where the search warrant is?

A. No, I cannot.

Q. Or what it recites?

A. No.[3]

Mahon posed the same general question to Sergeant Delau when he took the witness stand: "Will you tell us, officer, what happened when you arrived at [Dolly

Mapp's] home?"[4] Sergeant Delau testified under oath that Lieutenant White arrived at Mapp's home with a search warrant at about 4:00 P.M. Sergeant Delau contradicted Officer Haney's testimony in one respect though. Sergeant Delau admitted that the police pried open a screen door to gain entrance to the house.[5] Mahon did not call Lieutenant White to the stand to testify about the search warrant or to explain how the police got into Mapp's home. Nor did she produce the search warrant in court. Remember, though, the only question the jury had to decide was the factual one, whether Dolly Mapp possessed the obscene materials. On that issue, both officers testified that police had found all of the obscene materials in Mapp's bedroom, either in her dresser drawers or inside her suitcase.

Whether the police had lawfully entered Dolly Mapp's home, and the consequences if they had done so unlawfully, were strictly legal issues left for the judge to decide. The judge made this clear to the jurors in his instructions to them shortly before they retired to the jury room for deliberation of the case:

> At the outset the court should define for you what is meant by evidence, and how you are to weigh the testimony in this case. Throughout the course of the trial on occasion the court has ruled for or against the admission of evidence when objections were raised, either by the State or the defense. You will draw no

POLICE DEPARTMENT
CLEVELAND, OHIO

Melia
5-25-57

Bureau of Special Investigation

DEPARTMENTAL INFORMATION

EXAMINED BY *Melia Cooney* RANK Lieut.

May 23, 19 57
May 24, 19 57

FROM Carl I. Delau, Sgt. TO Martin P. Cooney, Lieut.

SUBJECT Arrest of DOLLREE MAPP, 14705 Milverton Ave., investigation in connec

COPIES TO Files, Detective Bur. tion with the malicious destruction of proper of Donald King, 3713 E. 151 St.

Sir:

In company with Patls. Dever #990 and Haney #258, at approximately 4:45 P.M. this date, arrested DOLLREE MAPP, also known as DOLLREE BIVINS, DOLLREE MOORE, 14705 Milverton Ave., F, C, age 29 and VERGIL OGLETREE, 1355 E.115 St. for investigation. Subject were conveyed to Central Station and booked at the Detective Bureau, to be photoed and printed.

Information was obtained from a confidential source which stated that a person wanted in connection with the bombing of Donald Kings home at 37 13 E. 151 St. was confining himself to this address and that there also was a lot of clearing house evidence at this location. This address of 14705 Milverton Ave. is the family brick home which has been known to be the property of the above Dollree Mapp with the subject residing on the second floor. Dollree Mapp had previous arrest for possession of clearinghouse slips M.C. 13.1318.

Checked 14705 Milverton Ave. at about 1:00 P.M. this date at which time we observed her auto parked in the garage. In the drive of this address we noticed an auto which is the property of Vergil Ogletree, MA-901, this person known to be a clearing house operator and had been connected with the operation of the California Gold policy when it was in operation. Detailed on this address until approximately 1:45 P.M. during which time neither Mapp or Ogletree left the premises. At this time we then made an effort to gain entrance to the residence of Mapp, on ringing the doorbell this subject would not come to the door but spoke to us through the second floor window. Mapp stated that she would not let us in unless we had a search warrant and said that she was the only person at home and that the woman who resides on the first floor was away for the day.

Remained in the vicinity of this home until a search warrant was obtained by Lieut. Thomas White who then came to this address. With the warrant in our possession we then gained entrance via the side door and found the above Dollree Mapp on the stairway between the first and second floor. Subject was placed under arrest and a search was made of the premises. In the basement we found a large foot locker which contained considerable policy paraphernalia, later examination showed that it contained the following, 5 sets of policy ball 1 marked chart sheet, 1 bundle of box car seals, one sealer, 14 bundles of California Gold day policy drawings, 14 bundles of Interstate day policy drawings, the California Gold drawings were of class 2247 thru 2260, the Interstate drawings were of class 2147 thru 2160. There were 7 bundles of California Gold night drawings, class 1124 to 1129, policy books, rubber bands and other equipment. This evidence was confiscated, tagged and turned in to the property room.

Made search of the second floor in company with Dollree Mapp and found the following which was confiscated and taken to Central Station. In one bedroom we found four books of a pornographics nature and several pictures, the books are titled as follows: London Stage Affairs, Affaire of a Troubadour, Memorirs of a Hotel Man, Littla Darlings. This evidence was found in a suitecase which is Dollree Mapps and contained evidence with her name on it.

POLICE DEPARTMENT
CLEVELAND, OHIO
DEPARTMENTAL INFORMATION

DIST. ZONE

EXAMINED BY RANK

FROM TO

SUBJECT Arrest of DOLLREE MAPP, 14705 Milverton Ave.

COPIES TO (continued)

In this same bedroom in a dresser drawer we found a weapon, a Cold make "Bronco" automatic, 7.65 MM, serial number 10410. This gun contained a magazine and no cartridges. Special report made on this gun and the weapon to be checked out by the Bureau of Scientific Identification.

In this same bedroom, various other photographs and material were confiscated including tapes for a tape recording machine. These will be played to determine if they contain anything of interest to this department.

From the kitchen of the second floor we confiscated policy books and pads and from a desk we confiscated three address books. Questioned Dollree Mapp while on the premises who stated that she resides on the second floor with her daughter Barbara Mapp, age 13 and Maurice Jones, age 26 and Margarette Cortes, age 22. These person were not on the premises and there was no clothing to indicate that they live at this address.

Made search of the first floor and in the kitchen we arrested Vergil Ogletree, this subject was searched but we failed to find any clearing house or policy evidence. This subject was seated in the kitchen with Minerva Fitzpatrik Lockheart, age 32. This person stated that she had lived at this address for 10 months and pays her rent to Dollree Mapp. Subject also stated that she was told by Mapp not to open the door for the police and for her to let Ogletree stay in her quarters.

At Central Station we requestioned Dollree Mapp, subject has no CPD photo number at present time. Subject stated that she has owned this home at 14705 Milverton for a year and nine months and had moved back to this address in Nov., 1956. She added that she collected rent of $100 per month from the woman on the first floor. Dollree Mapp has phone SK-2-3833 on the second floor listed to Dolores Moore, subject no longer resides at this address. Mapp denied that the obscene literature or policy evidence are hers. She stated that the Maurice Jones who moved away from her house five weeks ago had brought the foot locker to her home and that he also had left the obscene books behind when he left. Subject admits to being the girl friend of Edward Keeling who is a known clearing house figure. Mapp admitted to knowing Donald King and other clearing house figures but could give no help relative to the bombing of King's home. Subject is very evasive in her answers and was not making an effort to be helpful to the police.

Vergil Ogletree, our CPD #82226 was questioned at our office. This person admits to one arrest for clearing house violations but states that he has no connection with any clearing house or policy operations. He told us that he was at 14705 Milverton Ave. as he was picking up some cleaning and came to this address several minutes before the police. He denied that he had any connection with the clearing house business which was found in the basement. This subject stated that he had no information on the bombing and was home at the time.

Prosecutor to be consulted on the arrest of these two subjects.

Respectfully: *Carl D. Delau* Sgt.

This is a copy of the police report filed by Sargeant Carl Delau on May 24, 1957. It describes the search of Dolly Mapp's home and her subsequent arrest.

inference of any kind from any of the rulings of the court as on questions of law; neither will you because of any such rulings, or any other expression of the court, infer that the court has any opinion as to the guilt or innocence of the accused in this case . . .[6]

Judge Lybarger further instructed the jurors that in order to find Dolly Mapp guilty as charged in the indictment, they must find beyond a reasonable doubt that Mapp knowingly, that is voluntarily, had in her possession and under her control obscene books, pictures, and photographs. He explained that possession and control do not necessarily mean that the person owns the materials. He also explained the meaning of a very important legal term—"reasonable doubt":

> To doubt is to be honestly uncertain of the truth or of a fact; a reasonable doubt is a substantial doubt; it is not an unreasonable doubt; it is not a capricious doubt based merely upon conjecture, but it is a doubt based upon reason; it must be a doubt honestly uncertain and not a doubt originating in your mind from a desire to avoid the performance of a disagreeable duty; it is not a doubt created by any feeling of sympathy, passion or information not based upon the evidence in the case.[7]

The jury took only twenty minutes to consider all of the evidence and the judge's instructions. It found Dolly Mapp guilty as charged. The conviction, however, did not end Mahon's work on the case. She

Court of Appeals of Ohio, Eighth District, Cuyahoga County

State of Ohio,	January ___Term A. D. 19⁵⁹
Plaintiff-Appellee	
VS.	**Appeal from Common Pleas Court**
Dollree Mapp, a.k.a. Dolly Mapp	Appeal by Dollree Mapp, a.k.a. Dolly Mapp, Defendant-Appellant (LAW) C.A. 24,699 -- C.P. 68,326 Cr.
Defendant-Appellant	

This cause came on to be heard on the appeal on questions of law from the judgment of the Court of Common Pleas, and was argued by counsel for the parties. Defendant found guilty of violation of Section 2905.34 R.C. by the jury upon which judgment was entered. Defendant complains particularly of error in charge and complains of sentence imposed. Upon review of the entire case, we find no error prejudicial to the rights of the defendant. (Section 2945.83 R.C.). The question of punishment is within the exclusive jurisdiction of the trial court. The judgment of the Court of Common Pleas is therefore affirmed. It is ordered that appellee recover of appellant his costs herein taxed.

  It is ordered that a special mandate issue out of this Court directing the Court of Common Pleas to carry this judgment into execution. Appellant excepts.

  /s/ Joy Seth Hurd, Presiding Judge.

68326

00594

This copy of the decision of the Court of Appeals of Ohio affirms, or upholds, the trial court's judgment against Dolly Mapp.

continued to represent the State of Ohio in all of the subsequent appeals.

The Court of Appeals and the Supreme Court of Ohio agreed with Mahon's position on the two central issues in Mapp's case. Neither court found that the obscenity statute was unconstitutional and neither court overruled the *Lindway* case, which allowed the state of Ohio to present unlawfully seized evidence at trial. The decisions of those courts provided strong reinforcement for the legal arguments Mahon later presented to the United States Supreme Court.

The Supreme Court of Ohio had found that Dolly Mapp "not only took possession and control of the room which she had rented but also of the belongings of her former tenant, including the books and pictures which the undisputed evidence shows that she knew to be lewd and lascivious."[8] It also found that despite "considerable doubt as to whether there ever was any warrant for the search of defendant's home," there was no indication that the police had seized the evidence "by use of brutal or offensive physical force" against Mapp.[9]

Remember that up until that time, the United States Supreme Court had applied the exclusionary rule to the states only in a situation where the police had used physical force to remove evidence from a defendant's person (*Rochin* v. *California*). Because the police

did not forcibly remove the obscene materials from
Dolly Mapp's person, the Ohio Supreme Court clung
to its *Lindway* case. It held that Judge Lybarger was correct when he allowed the prosecutor to introduce the
seized evidence at trial.

In contrast to the ease with which the Ohio
Supreme Court upheld the introduction of the seized
evidence, the constitutionality of the obscenity statute
was a close call for Mahon. Four of the seven Justices
believed the statute was unconstitutional. Those
Justices recognized that the statute required the jury to
convict Mapp even if it believed that the obscene materials belonged to someone else, that she did not intend
to look at them again, and that she was merely storing
them for Morris Jones. According to the four Justices,
to require a jury to convict a defendant under those circumstances would mean that law-abiding people
would be discouraged from even looking at books and
pictures—an effect that the Justices believed clearly violated the freedom of speech and press guaranteed by the
First and Fourteenth Amendments to the United States
Constitution.[10]

Even though the majority of the Justices voted to
overturn the statute, a mere majority vote was not
enough to overturn a statute under Ohio law. Ohio law
required agreement by at least six of the seven Justices

on the court before a statute could be declared unconstitutional. In the end, Mahon's position prevailed, and the obscenity statute remained in force in Ohio.

Dolly Mapp and her attorneys did not stop there, however. By filing a *Petition for Writ of Certiorari* they asked the United States Supreme Court to hear the case, and the Court agreed to do so. Mahon had to prepare a written response (a brief in opposition) on behalf of the State of Ohio.

There are several important sections to every brief filed in the United States Supreme Court. Those sections include a jurisdictional statement, a statement of facts, legal arguments, and a conclusion. The jurisdictional statement certifies that the petitioner has exhausted all other state court remedies and that the case properly comes before the Supreme Court. The statement of facts is a summary of the trial testimony. It cites the actual trial transcripts, the written record of the trial testimony. In the statement of facts each party tells the story of what happened at trial from its own perspective, pointing out facts that support its legal argument, but it is very important that the statement of facts be accurate and truthful.

For example, Mahon's brief highlighted Officer Haney's testimony that the police had a search warrant when they arrived at Dolly Mapp's house and that Mapp permitted the police to enter her home. Kearns, on the other hand, highlighted Sergeant Delau's testimony that the police pried open the door, as well as Mapp's testimony that the police were rough with her and did not permit her to read the piece of paper they claimed was a search warrant. Mahon's brief related the police officers' testimony that all of the obscene materials were found inside Dolly Mapp's bedroom, while Kearns pointed out Mapp's testimony that the materials were packed in a box in the basement. Each of those factual presentations formed the basis for each party's legal arguments.

Mahon's first legal argument was that the obscenity statute was constitutional. According to Mahon, the obvious intent of the statute prohibiting possession of obscene materials was to prevent the circulation or distribution of those materials to other persons. Mahon did not see any difference between a bookseller who possesses obscene literature in his store and a private citizen like Mapp who knows that she possesses obscene materials in her home. The statute, Mahon argued, was designed to cover all persons who possess obscene materials. The reason for that, Mahon asserted, was to prevent the person who possessed the materials from circulating them.

Mahon also responded to Mapp's argument that the evidence should have been excluded because the police seized it unlawfully. Mahon argued that the exclusionary rule did not apply in Ohio because of the *Lindway* case. Mahon knew that Mapp's brief highlighted Ohio Supreme Court Justice Herbert's dissenting opinion. Remember that Justice Herbert wanted to modify the *Lindway* rule in this particular case. Even though Justice Herbert's opinion was not the opinion of the majority of the Justices, Mahon responded to Mapp's argument by confronting Justice Herbert's opinion head on.

Mrs. Mahon did not agree with Justice Herbert's opinion and she stated so in her brief to the United States Supreme Court. She pointed out that the police did not know that Mapp possessed the obscene material until they found it inside her home. Mahon wrote, "The constitutional guarantee against unreasonable searches and seizures was never meant to prevent the administration of criminal justice. It speaks of the right of the people to be secure in their persons, houses, papers, and effects. Nothing is said in that provision guaranteeing security and immunity in the commission of crimes."[11]

Having read all of the briefs filed in the case, the Supreme Court scheduled oral arguments for March 29, 1961. This would be Dolly Mapp's last chance to convince the Court that her conviction should be reversed.

5

The Supreme Court Decides

Dolly Mapp sat in the spectator section of the imposing, marble courtroom as the nine Justices of the United States Supreme Court took their seats to listen to oral arguments in the case of *Mapp* v. *Ohio.* She had traveled to Washington, D.C., from Cleveland, Ohio, intent on witnessing the Supreme Court decide what would later become a landmark case.

Since the Supreme Court was formed, it has been customary during oral arguments for the Chief Justice to sit at the center of the bench. On March 29, 1961, Chief Justice Earl Warren was surrounded by Justices Hugo L. Black; Felix Frankfurter; William O. Douglas; Tom C. Clark; John M. Harlan, II; William J.

Brennan, Jr.; Charles E. Whittaker; and Potter Stewart. Who were these nine men and how would their views affect the outcome of Dolly Mapp's case?

The Justices were known for rendering sharply split decisions. Justice Black, a former Alabama senator and once a member of the Ku Klux Klan, was a staunch liberal (not narrow in opinion or judgment) and clear leader of the liberal minority, which included Chief Justice Warren and Justices Douglas and Brennan. Justice Frankfurter, a brilliant former Harvard law professor and one of only five foreign-born Justices who had ever served on the Supreme Court, was the leader of the conservative Justices (those Justices who were inclined to maintain existing views and conditions.) Justice Frankfurter believed that the Court should not decide cases merely to express an opinion. That is, it should not take an active role in changing laws, which he believed only legislators should change. Justice Black, on the other hand, believed that the Court should take an active role in protecting individuals' rights.

The United States Supreme Court begins a new term each year on the first Monday in October. Often the cases it hears reflect political and social controversies of the time. During the 1960–61 term, when the Supreme Court heard Dolly Mapp's case, John F. Kennedy was

The United States Supreme Court begins a new term each year on the first Monday in October. The interior chambers of the United States Supreme Court are shown here.

president of the United States. His brother, Robert F. Kennedy, was attorney general.

The country was embroiled in a variety of legal battles in the early 1960s. The Department of Justice was actively investigating suspected Communists. Business owners were up in arms about newly enacted "Blue Laws" that prevented them from opening their businesses on Sunday. Alabama had changed a city's boundaries in order to deprive African Americans of the right to vote in certain elections. Louisiana had tried to enact laws to get around a federal court order to desegregate the public schools. Consequently, by the beginning of the October 1960 term, a number of major cases had made their way to the Supreme Court. The same nine Justices who heard Dolly Mapp's case were called upon to decide those cases.

Despite the Court's full agenda, at noon on March 29, 1961, the Court turned its attention to the issues presented in *Mapp* v. *Ohio*. Dolly Mapp's attorney, Alexander Kearns, then sixty-six years old, was the first to speak to the Court. In their book, *The Constitution: That Delicate Balance*, authors Fred Friendly and Martha Elliott described Kearns as having "all the bravado of a Clarence Darrow and the inflection of W.C. Fields" as he recited the facts of the case to the Justices.[1]

Kearns began by telling the Court that the Cleveland police officers entered Dolly Mapp's home with a piece of paper that they claimed was a search warrant but that there was, in fact, no search warrant. Shortly after he began though, Justice Frankfurter seemed a little bored. He asked Kearns, "May I trouble you to tell us what do you deem to be the questions that are open before this [C]ourt?"[2] Justice Frankfurter was particularly interested in knowing whether Kearns was asking the Court to consider the legality of the search and seizure issue.

Kearns emphatically replied that the search and seizure was indeed at issue. To make his point, he described Ohio's *Lindway* case, which allowed the use of illegally seized evidence in a criminal trial, as "advocating anarchy."[3] Justice Frankfurter pressed him again. This time, Justice Frankfurter wanted to discuss the Supreme Court's 1949 decision in *Wolf* v. *Colorado*. (In that case the Supreme Court refused to apply the exclusionary rule to the states. The Court acknowledged however, that the due process clause in the Fourteenth Amendment, an amendment that applies to the states, contained the same guarantees as the right against unreasonable searches and seizures in the Fourth Amendment, which does not apply to the states.) What followed was this dialogue between Justice Frankfurter and Mr. Kearns:

> **Frankfurter:** Are you asking us to overrule the *Wolf* case in this court? I notice it isn't even cited in your brief. I just want to know what is before us, Mr. Kearns . . . So far as I can make out that question isn't here, is it?
>
> **Kearns:** Yes it is . . .
>
> **Frankfurter:** But it wasn't decided by your court.
>
> **Kearns:** It was raised in our court but of course they didn't actually decide it by putting it in the syllabus [the Court's opinion].[4]

Surprisingly, Kearns seemed unfamiliar with the *Wolf* case. His further responses suggested that he and Justice Frankfurter were talking about two different issues. Justice Frankfurter had asked about the *Wolf* case. Kearns's response, however, had nothing to do with the *Wolf* case. Instead, he began to talk about one of the other issues he had raised in his brief—why he believed the trial judge had erred when he instructed the jury at the end of the trial. At one point, without discussing the Court's holding in the *Wolf* case, Kearns commented that he thought the State of Ohio would have cited the *Wolf* case in its brief.

Kearns's responses were not satisfactory. Another Justice wanted to know whether Kearns's client was asking the Court to overrule *Wolf* v. *Colorado*. That time Kearns responded, "No. I don't believe we are."[5]

If Kearns did not want the Court to overrule *Wolf*, then how could the Court rule in Dolly Mapp's case that the illegally seized evidence was inadmissible? The *Wolf* case specifically stated that the exclusionary rule did not apply to state criminal trials. Did Kearns's response end all hope for Mapp that the Court would reconsider the *Wolf* case?

We can only speculate whether Kearns's response would have ended the discussion of whether the Court should overrule *Wolf* and extend the exclusionary rule to the states. His response did not end the discussion in Dolly Mapp's case because the Court had also allowed the ACLU to share the time allotted for oral argument on behalf of Mapp. ACLU attorney Bernard Berkman was quite clear about the position of his organization:

> The American Civil Liberties Union and its Ohio affiliate . . . [are] very clear as to the question directed toward the appellant that we are asking this court to reconsider *Wolf* v. *Colorado* and to find that evidence that is unlawfully and illegally obtained should not be permitted into a state proceeding and its production is a violation of the federal constitution's Fourth and Fourteenth Amendment. We have no hesitancy in asking the Court to reconsider it because we think that it is a necessary part of due process.[6]

Next it was Mahon's turn to present her oral argument on behalf of the State of Ohio. She began with the Ohio obscenity statute. Mahon argued that the statute was not overly broad as Kearns had contended in his brief. To make her point more forcefully, Mahon told the United States Supreme Court Justices that she disagreed with her own state's Supreme Court in one important respect.

The Ohio Supreme Court had interpreted the obscenity statute to require the jury to convict Dolly Mapp even if the jury believed that the obscene materials belonged to Morris Jones and were stored in the basement, as Mapp had testified. Mahon, on the other hand, interpreted the statute to mean that if a defendant had possession of obscene materials *for someone else*, the defendant did not have control over those materials. According to Mahon's interpretation, if the jury had believed Ms. Mapp's testimony about the obscene materials, it would have found her not guilty. Therefore, Mahon asserted, the jury obviously did not believe Mapp's testimony that Morris Jones owned the materials, and that she had stored them for him in the basement. She also argued to the Court that the purpose of the statute, although it did not specifically state so, was to prevent circulation of obscene materials.

Mahon interpreted Ohio law as supporting her view that the statute was not overly broad. She believed that a situation could exist in which a person could have obscene materials in his or her house but not be in criminal possession of those materials under the law. The ultimate effect of the statute, though, seemed to bother Justice Frankfurter, especially because it punished mere possession of obscene materials. He engaged Mahon in this somewhat humorous dialogue:

> **Frankfurter:** Let me see if I understand—it means any book on my shelves, any of my shelves, . . . found to be obscene, constitutes a possession. He does nothing but have it on his shelf . . .
>
> **Mahon:** A knowing possession under this statute, a knowing possession of obscenity is prohibited by this statute . . . I would say it extends to anybody who had . . .
>
> **Frankfurter:** On his book shelf, merely a part of his library. He's a bibliophile and he collects first editions, not for the content, but because they are first editions. Any book on his shelf—my shelf—which I know to be obscene in content, a matter of great indifference to me because I'm interested in the fact that it was published in 1527. That makes me . . . a violator of this statute. Is that correct?
>
> **Mahon:** I would say so, your Honor. Any collection of obscenity would be . . .
>
> (Laughter heard in the courtroom)
>
> **Frankfurter:** Mark Twain had one of the biggest collections, and I could tell you now where it is, but it's outside your jurisdiction.

(Laughter heard in the courtroom)

But . . . you said that the purpose of this—the aim of this statute is to prevent circulation, dissemination. Now, having it on a shelf isn't disseminating it, quite the opposite. There are no more miserly people in the world than bibliophiles.[7]

Mahon argued that anyone who possessed obscene materials would have the opportunity to circulate them. She admitted, though, that Dolly Mapp had not been charged with attempting to circulate the books and pictures. Nevertheless, Mahon urged the Justices to uphold the statute.

A pivotal discussion followed on the issue of the search warrant. It would play a significant role in the outcome of Dolly Mapp's case. For it was during this portion of the oral argument that the prosecutor admitted for the first time, on the record, that *the police did not have a search warrant to seize obscene materials at Dolly Mapp's home on May 23, 1957*. Despite the trial testimony of Sergeant Delau and Officer Haney, Mahon advised the nine Justices of the United States Supreme Court that the search warrant did not exist. She admitted that the search was unlawful.

Mahon's admission did not change the thrust of her legal argument though. She still insisted that the obscene materials were admissible at Mapp's trial even though the police had seized them without a valid search warrant. Her reasoning was the same as it had been all along.

As Mahon explained to the Justices, Ohio did not have an exclusionary rule at the time. Under the *Lindway* case, Ohio law permitted unlawfully seized evidence to be presented at trial. Mahon argued:

> The absence of a search warrant can be no defense to a crime. If the evidence establishes the crime what defense is there in the absence of a search warrant? It's a collateral matter [a side issue for which there is another remedy.] It provides for a civil suit for trespass if that constitutional right is violated.[8]

When Mahon had completed her argument, the Court permitted Kearns an opportunity for rebuttal, that is, a chance to respond to Mahon's arguments. This time, Kearns was more prepared to discuss *Wolf* v. *Colorado.*

Kearns presented the Court with an alternative to overruling *Wolf* v. *Colorado.* He argued that where there is "real criminality," that is, where a defendant is truly guilty of a crime, then the *Wolf* case and the *Lindway* case should still apply. In those cases, unlawfully seized evidence would be admissible at a criminal trial in Ohio under the *Lindway* rule, but it would not be admissible in a federal trial under the *Wolf* rule.

However, Kearns urged the United States Supreme Court to rule that unlawfully seized evidence was not

The nine Supreme Court Justices who heard the *Mapp* case are shown here. The Justices seated in the bottom row, from left to right, are William O. Douglas; Hugo L. Black; Earl Warren; Felix Frankfurter; and Tom C. Clark. Those standing, from left to right, are Charles E. Whittaker; John M. Harlan, II; William J. Brennan, Jr.; and Potter Stewart.

admissible in a state criminal trial in a case where the defendant did not intend to break the law and the public was not injured by the defendant's crime. According to Kearns, Dolly Mapp's trial clearly established that she had no intent to violate the Ohio obscenity statute, and she had not injured the public by storing obscene materials in her basement.

The oral argument lasted two hours—twice as long as most oral arguments before the Supreme Court. After hearing each party's views, the nine Justices retired to their chambers to consider the case. Dolly Mapp returned to Cleveland to await the decision about whether she would have to go to jail. During an interview more than twenty years later, in the summer of 1983, Mapp described a conversation that she had with one of the Court bailiffs shortly before she left the courtroom. According to Mapp, she asked the bailiff,

> "How long before I can expect a decision?" And he said, "Oh, months, months, months." . . . And I said, . . . "You should call me. Really you should call me collect." He said, "Well, you know they only come down on Monday." . . . And every Monday I waited and every Monday he called. That thirteenth Monday, he called and he said, "Dollree, you don't have to go to jail. It's all over." That's the way he said it to me. That's all I heard.[9]

The bailiff was right. Dolly Mapp would not have to go to jail. The Supreme Court had reversed her

criminal trial. He believed the evidence should have been admissible at the federal trial.

No one knows exactly what happened between the time the Justices agreed that the Ohio obscenity statute was unconstitutional and the actual written decision. Justice Potter Stewart later said:

> I have always suspected that the members of the soon-to-be *Mapp* majority had met in what I affectionately call a 'rump caucus' to discuss a different basis for the decision. But regardless of how they reached their decision, five Justices of the Court concluded that Dolly Mapp's conviction had to be reversed because evidence seized in an illegal search had to be excluded from state as well as federal trials. *Wolf* v. *Colorado* was to be overruled.[11]

On June 19, 1961, the United States Supreme Court delivered its opinion. The five to four majority reversed Dolly Mapp's conviction and held that all evidence seized in violation of the Constitution was no longer admissible in a state criminal trial. The Court overruled *Wolf* v. *Colorado*.

Justice Clark, writing for the majority, noted that one of the reasons the *Wolf* court had refused to apply the exclusionary rule in state criminal proceedings was because the states were designing other ways of protecting an individual's right to privacy. (Remember that some states had allowed lawsuits for money damages against law enforcement officers who violated the Constitution, and other states provided for criminal sanctions against those officers.) Between the 1949 *Wolf* decision and the *Mapp* case, however, more than half of the states that were initially opposed to an exclusionary rule had in fact adopted it. As a California court noted, "other remedies have completely failed to secure compliance with the constitutional provisions. . . ."[12] The *Mapp* Court was now ready to protect an individual's right to privacy directly through the use of the Constitution.

The *Wolf* court had already held that the Fourth Amendment right of privacy could be enforced against the states through the Due Process Clause of the Fourteenth Amendment. That theory was known as the incorporation doctrine. The only remaining step was to extend the exclusionary rule, already in force in federal court proceedings, to state court proceedings. The *Mapp* Court was now ready to take this next step.

Justice Clark believed that applying the exclusionary rule to the states "makes very good sense." He gave an example of how illogical the law was in 1961:

> Presently, a federal prosecutor may make no use of evidence illegally seized, but a State's attorney across the street may, although he supposedly is operating under the enforceable prohibitions of the same Amendment. Thus the State, by admitting evidence unlawfully seized, serves to encourage disobedience to

the Federal Constitution which it is bound to uphold."[13]

Mapp now made this double standard unacceptable. The Court knew that some people would criticize the decision. As Justice Benjamin Cardozo once wrote, the result of the exclusionary rule is that "[t]he criminal is to go free because the constable has blundered."[14] Justice Clark realized that in some cases, that would be true. But his written opinion encouraged a different view: "The criminal goes free, if he must, but it is the law that sets him free. Nothing can destroy a government more quickly than its failure to observe its own laws, or worse, its disregard of the charter of its own existence."[15]

The Supreme Court would not permit the basic right to privacy "to be revocable at the whim of any police officer who, in the name of law enforcement itself, chooses to suspend its enjoyment."[16] Otherwise, the Fourth Amendment would be reduced to a "form of words."[17]

Justices Hugo L. Black and William O. Douglas, both part of the majority, wrote separate concurring opinions. Justice Black, who had once agreed with the *Wolf* Court that the exclusionary rule should not be enforced in state court proceedings, now found that the exclusionary rule was necessary. But he was the only Justice to reach that conclusion by using both the Fourth and

Fifth Amendments, as the Supreme Court had done in the *Boyd* case in 1886.

Justice Potter Stewart, who had written the majority opinion in *Elkins*, refused to join the majority in the *Mapp* opinion. He did not think that Dolly Mapp's attorneys had properly briefed or argued the search and seizure issue. However, he concluded that Mapp's conviction should have been reversed—not because of the search warrant issue but because, in his opinion, the Ohio obscenity statute was unconstitutional.

The three remaining Justices—Harlan, Frankfurter, and Whittaker—dissented. Justice Harlan, writing for the dissenting Justices, highlighted the fact that the central issue on appeal was the constitutionality of the Ohio statute, not the search and seizure issue. He suggested that the majority had simply "reached out" to overrule the *Wolf* case but had "no justification for regarding this case as an appropriate occasion for re-examining *Wolf*."[18] The search and seizure issue, in the view of the three dissenting Justices, "was briefed not at all and argued only extremely tangentially [meaning that the issue was only touched upon but not briefed in detail.]"[19]

The dissenting Justices also did not approve of the majority's reasons for extending the exclusionary rule to the states. Most importantly, they rejected the majority's theory that the Fourteenth Amendment incorporated not only the right to privacy guaranteed by the Fourth Amendment, but also the federal remedy for violations of that right—the exclusionary rule. The dissenters believed that the remedy should be left for the states to decide.

The majority decision in *Mapp* v. *Ohio* became the law of the land. The exclusionary rule would now be applied in every criminal court, state or federal, throughout the United States.

One issue still remained a mystery. Prosecutor Mahon had told the Supreme Court Justices during her oral argument that the police did not have a search warrant to seize obscene materials from Dolly Mapp's home. But Sergeant Delau and Officer Michael Haney had testified at Mapp's trial that Lieutenant White obtained a search warrant. Mapp had testified that the lieutenant showed her a piece of paper that he claimed was the search warrant but he would not let her read it. Was there ever a search warrant of any kind?

Twenty-two years after the *Mapp* decision, in the summer of 1983, Sergeant Carl Delau described during an interview what had really happened on May 23, 1957:

> When the lieutenant went to get the search warrant . . .
> he went to the prosecutors and got a proper affidavit.
> He went to the clerk's office and had it signed, went
> to a judge, got a judge's signature. . . . He walked out

with the affidavit. . . . He only got an affidavit! He never got a warrant. And as a result, when I finally looked at it outside the scene, and I seen [sic] it was just an affidavit . . . I wasn't going to make an issue over it. . . . So, were we going to say we only had the affidavit?[20]

What happened to Dolly Mapp after the landmark Supreme Court decision? Unfortunately, her four-year odyssey to the Supreme Court was not her last experience with the criminal justice system. Not long after the decision, Mapp moved to New York to open a furniture store. One day the local police knocked on her door just as they had done years ago in Cleveland. But this time was different. When Dolly Mapp opened the door, the officer said to her, "We have a search warrant this time." Mapp had no choice but to let them in.

As a result of the search, in 1973 Mapp was convicted of possession of illegal narcotics. Under a New York law she was sentenced to serve twenty years to life in prison. She was paroled after nine years, four months, and seventeen days.[21] After her release from prison, she worked for a time as a legal aide for prison inmates.[22] Dolly Mapp is now in her sixties and works as a real estate and insurance agent in New York.[23]

In the years following *Mapp* v. *Ohio*, the decision generated enormous controversy throughout the country. Those who defended the decision argued that suppressing illegally seized evidence would deter police misconduct; those who opposed the decision argued that the exclusionary rule was not a deterrent because it did not directly punish the officers who acted improperly.

In 1963 the Supreme Court extended the exclusionary rule to include any evidence that was indirectly the product of unlawful police conduct or "fruit of the poisonous tree." The holding in *Wong Sun* v. *United States* meant that if unlawfully seized evidence led police to other incriminating evidence, that evidence was also inadmissible because it was the "fruit of the poisonous tree."[24]

Although the likelihood of abolishing the exclusionary rule was slim so long as the same Justices remained on the bench, three of the Justices were in their seventies and were nearing retirement. Who would take their places, and would the new Justices agree with the opponents of the exclusionary rule? Much would depend on who was president of the United States at the time the Justices retired, since it is the president who appoints Supreme Court Justices to the bench.

During the next three decades, a mixture of tragedy, politics, and public opinion would alter the course of Fourth Amendment law in the United States. The *Mapp* v. *Ohio* decision was destined for rocky roads.

6

The Future of the Exclusionary Rule

Certain events, sometimes tragic ones, can alter the course of history. One such event was the assassination of President John F. Kennedy on November 22, 1963. While no one could have predicted with certainty whether he would have been elected to a second term of office, his untimely death undeniably affected the future of politics in America. The liberal thinking of the 1960s—which encouraged restrictions on the authority of police officers—gave way to a gradual shift to more conservative views. These views fought to maintain, and in some instances, give more authority to police officers during the thirty years following President Kennedy's assassination. Americans voted for

Republican presidents like Richard Nixon, Gerald Ford, Ronald Reagan, and George Bush, who cumulatively held office for twenty years. Those presidents nominated federal judges who influenced the judicial branch. The voters began to change the composition of the United States Senate and House of Representatives from a majority of Democrats to a majority of Republicans. Recently, Congress has been pushing for reforms in welfare and affirmative action programs that date back to the 1960s.

The gradual shift to conservativism has particularly affected another arena—the United States Supreme Court. Historically, Republican presidents have appointed conservatives to the Supreme Court while Democrat presidents have appointed liberal thinkers. As elder Justices retired from service, the Republican presidents who held office during the twenty years since the *Mapp* v. *Ohio* case filled vacancies with several persons known for their conservative legal views. The effect of those appointments on the course of the law in many areas, including search and seizure law, has been dramatic.

During the late 1960s, the Court created several exceptions to the requirement that a police officer have a warrant before a search is conducted. For example, the Court held in *Chimel* v. *California* that, in order to protect the safety of the police officer and prevent a suspect from destroying evidence, a police officer may search an arrestee and the area within that person's immediate control.[1] A police officer may also stop and search a moving vehicle without a warrant if there is cause to believe a crime has been committed and that evidence will be found inside the vehicle.[2] In addition, no warrant is necessary to enter a suspect's home if the police are in hot pursuit of the suspect.[3]

Opposition to the exclusionary rule became a driving force behind several Supreme Court decisions in the 1970s and 1980s. With a new Chief Justice, Warren E. Burger, and three new associate Justices, all of whom were appointed by President Nixon, the interests of law enforcement emerged. In *United States* v. *Calandra*, decided in 1974, Justice Lewis F. Powell wrote that the exclusionary rule was not a constitutional right of privacy.[4] Although a defendant's Fourth Amendment rights are violated when a police officer conducts an unlawful search, that is, a search without a warrant when one is necessary, or a search with a warrant that is invalid, the admission of unlawfully seized evidence "work[s] no new Fourth Amendment wrong."[5] Rather, according to the majority, "the rule's prime purpose is to deter future unlawful police conduct."[6] Justice Powell reasoned that if the rule were meant only to deter police misconduct, then the Court should balance the deterrent benefits against the social costs—if exclusion of illegally seized evidence was not likely to result in deterring police misconduct it would be admissible. Therefore, the Court decided that the exclusionary rule should not be applied to evidence used in a grand jury proceeding.

Later rulings by the Supreme Court continued to use the costs-and-benefits analysis developed in *Calandra*. The Court held that unlawfully seized evidence is admissible in federal civil cases and in deportation hearings involving illegal aliens.[7] Unlawfully seized evidence that is inadmissible in the prosecution's case-in-chief, the portion of the government's case where it presents its own witnesses and evidence, may be used solely to impeach—test the credibility of—a defendant who testifies in a criminal trial.[8] Suppression of evidence is also not required where the search was made in reliance on a criminal statute that is valid at the time of the search though later declared unconstitutional.[9]

The shift in the thinking of the Supreme Court also brought about several new exceptions to the exclusionary rule. These would allow prosecutors to use unlawfully seized evidence during their presentation of the government's case in a criminal trial. In 1984, the Court heard the case of *Nix* v. *Williams*.[10] Robert

Williams was convicted of first-degree murder in the death of ten-year-old Pamela Powers. While in police custody, Williams directed the officers to the location where he had hidden Pamela's body. The jury found Williams guilty as charged, but the Supreme Court later reversed the conviction and ordered a new trial because the police had violated Williams's Sixth Amendment right to counsel. The police had promised Williams's lawyer they would not interrogate him when, in fact, they asked him to think about telling them where the body was so the child's parents could give her a Christian burial. Therefore, the Court held that although Williams's statements were inadmissible at his second trial, any evidence discovered as a result of those statements to the police may have been admissible on a theory of inevitable discovery.

During Williams's second trial, the prosecutor did not offer into evidence Williams's statements about where the body would be found. However, the trial court did admit evidence of the condition of the body as police found it in a ditch, articles of the child's clothing, and results of medical tests on the body. Williams was convicted for the second time; again he appealed his conviction.

Chief Justice Burger, a staunch opponent of the exclusionary rule, wrote the opinion for the majority.

The Court held that evidence is properly admitted at trial if the evidence would inevitably have been discovered even if no constitutional violation had occurred. In the *Williams* case, a search party of two hundred persons had already been looking for Pamela Powers's body. The trial court concluded that because the body was within the area to be searched, the search team would inevitably have discovered the body in the same condition as it was when Mr. Williams led the police to it. Therefore, Chief Justice Burger wrote, it "would reject logic, experience, and common sense" to apply the exclusionary rule. The defendant had suffered no prejudice, and the State had gained no advantage over the defendant because the body would have been discovered regardless of whether Williams had told the police where it was located.

The "inevitable discovery" rule is similar to, but not exactly the same as, the "independent source" doctrine, another exception to the exclusionary rule. That doctrine allows the admission of evidence that has been discovered through a wholly independent source, which means it was discovered separately from any unlawful police conduct. For example, suppose a prosecutor agrees to grant immunity from prosecution to a witness who gives incriminating testimony in a *state* criminal trial about matters related to a *federal* prosecution. The law prevents federal authorities from admitting those statements against the witness if the witness is prosecuted in federal court for the federal crime. In order to prosecute the witness for his or her admitted participation in a federal crime, the federal authorities must obtain evidence of the witness's criminal activities from a totally separate source (for example, an eye witness who saw that person committing the crime).

The Supreme Court created another exception to the exclusionary rule in 1984, the same year it decided *Nix* v. *Williams*. In *United States* v. *Leon*, the Court held that the exclusionary rule does not apply to evidence obtained by police officers who reasonably rely on a search warrant that is later found to be defective.[11] Known as the "good-faith exception," it allows unlawfully seized evidence to be admitted in criminal prosecutions if the police made an honest mistake in obtaining a search warrant.

Search warrants must be authorized by a judge or magistrate. The process begins when a police officer submits a sworn affidavit showing that there is probable cause to believe that evidence of a crime will be found at the place to be searched. Before the judge or magistrate can properly issue the search warrant, he or she must determine that the affidavit does establish probable cause. In *Leon*, the magistrate issued a search warrant based upon a police officer's affidavit. It was later determined, however, that although the police had conducted a lengthy investigation into the alleged drug trafficking activities of the defendant, the officer who prepared the affidavit in support of the search warrant neglected to include important facts that would establish probable cause. The magistrate had erred in finding probable cause to issue the search warrant.

Justice Byron White again wrote that the purpose of the exclusionary rule is to deter police misconduct. But when the police obtain a warrant that they reasonably believe is valid, "there is no police illegality and thus nothing to deter."[12] "Penalizing the officer for the magistrate's error, rather than his own, cannot logically contribute to the deterrence of Fourth Amendment violations."[13] Justice White cautioned, however, that if a police officer knowingly provides false information to the magistrate, or if the warrant is so deficient on its face that the police officer should have known it was invalid, then suppression of the evidence is still an appropriate remedy.

The Reagan administration and law enforcement agencies were very pleased with the Supreme Court's ruling. An administration official was quoted as saying: "It restores a better balance to the criminal justice system."[14] An Atlanta district attorney noted that "this ruling takes the technicality out and gives us more practicality, and that's what we need."[15]

It appears that the controversies surrounding the exclusionary rule and the direction of the Supreme Court will continue for years to come. In 1995, the Supreme Court again addressed the appropriateness of the exclusionary rule in *Arizona* v. *Evans.*[16] Chief Justice William Rehnquist, appointed as Chief Justice in 1986, reiterated the Court's position that the exclusionary rule is an appropriate remedy to a Fourth Amendment violation only in those cases where exclusion of unlawfully seized evidence will deter police misconduct. In *Arizona,* the police officer reasonably relied on a police computer record that was later found to contain a court clerk's error. The Supreme Court noted that exclusion of the evidence in that instance would not serve the purpose of the exclusionary rule because there was no police misconduct and the exclusionary rule was designed to deter police misconduct, not judicial mistakes.

Although the Supreme Court has created many exceptions to the exclusionary rule since the days of *Mapp* v. *Ohio,* it is questionable whether the Court will ultimately abolish the rule. While the Court has had many opportunities to do so since the *Mapp* decision,

It is still unknown whether the Supreme Court will ultimately abolish the exclusionary rule.

it continues to uphold the basic rule as a remedy to Fourth Amendment violations. The *Arizona* v. *Evans* decision, however, still emphasizes that the exclusionary rule is not a constitutional right. It is merely a judicially created remedy for a violation of a Fourth Amendment right. That may leave room in the future for the Court to abolish the rule entirely.

The United States Supreme Court is not the only entity that can have a significant effect on the future of the exclusionary rule, however. Remember that Congress can pass a law that affects the use of the rule. In fact, on February 8, 1995, the House of Representatives passed Bill HR 666, authored by Representative Bill McCollum (R.-Fla.). The bill allows evidence to be admitted in a federal criminal trial if the police reasonably believed that the search conformed with the requirements of the Fourth Amendment. In other words, if the police officer acted in good faith in seizing the evidence, the evidence is admissible at trial even if the seizure violated the defendant's Fourth Amendment rights. The bill provides for monetary awards for those persons who were physically injured or sustained property damage as a result of an unconstitutional search.

The future of the exclusionary rule is still unknown. Some would like to see the rule abolished entirely.

Many politicians and legal scholars, however, are strongly opposed to weakening the rule. Whether *Mapp* v. *Ohio* will remain in force in the future will certainly depend on the political influences. How the United States Supreme Court and Congress will respond to these opposing views is yet to be seen.

Questions for Discussion

1. Sometime in the near future Congress may pass a law abolishing the exclusionary rule. You are a senior attorney for the American Civil Liberties Union and have been invited to testify before the Senate Judiciary Committee. This is the committee that will eventually decide the fate of the exclusionary rule. What arguments will you make to persuade the committee that the exclusionary rule is necessary to our system of criminal justice? How will you respond to a senator's comment that the exclusionary rule only protects criminals?

2. You are an assistant prosecutor. You have just learned that two police officers raided an elderly woman's home without a valid search warrant. During

the search, the officers discovered some sleeping pills in Mrs. Jones's nightstand by her bed. She did not have a doctor's prescription for the pills. The officers explain that their most reliable informant had told them that a person who was suspected of kidnapping was hiding in the house where Jones lived. The officers obtained a search warrant for Jones's home based on the information they received from their informant. To their surprise, they later learned that they had made a mistake. The suspected kidnapper had been hiding in the house next door to Jones's house, not inside her house. You have been assigned to prosecute Jones for illegal possession of narcotics. Jones's defense attorney argues that the evidence (the pills) was unlawfully seized because the search warrant was based on false information. How do you counter the defense attorney's argument and try to convince the judge to allow you to introduce the evidence against Jones at her trial?

3. The exclusionary rule does not apply to grand jury proceedings. That means that even if the police seize evidence unlawfully, the evidence can be considered by the grand jury in determining whether there is probable cause to prosecute the accused. Should the exclusionary rule apply to grand jury proceedings? Why or why not?

4. You and your family are at home one evening watching television together. Suddenly five police officers break down your front door and enter your house with their guns drawn. They handcuff you and your family, including your elderly grandmother, who faints from the excitement and bumps her head against the wall. The police search every nook and cranny in every room. They empty drawers onto the floor, toss clothes from the closets, tear down pictures hanging on the walls, and cut the sofa cushions in half. Two hours later, while you are still handcuffed in the living room, an officer finds one marijuana joint under your mattress. He places you under arrest for possession of marijuana. You ask to see the search warrant, but he laughs and tells you that technically he does not really need a search warrant because the new law states that evidence is admissible even if he does not have a search warrant. Have the officers acted improperly in any respect? After you are tried and convicted, what remedies do you propose to Congress and to your state legislature to compensate private citizens for police misconduct?

5. It is the year 2050. The medical profession has designed a new surgical procedure that will enable neurosurgeons (brain surgeons) to determine what you are thinking. What arguments can be made under the

Fourth and Fifth Amendments to suppress any evidence of a crime the police obtain by forcing a suspected criminal to undergo this new surgery?

6. If Congress abolishes the exclusionary rule, should there be any exceptions? If so, under what circumstances should the Courts prevent the government from introducing illegally seized evidence at a criminal trial? If not, why not?

7. Discuss the reasons you believe that *Mapp* v. *Ohio* has not been overruled by the United States Supreme Court despite the newly created exceptions to the exclusionary rule.

Chapter Notes

Chapter 1

1. "5 Now Held in Bombing of King's Home," *Cleveland Plain Dealer*, May 21, 1957, pp. 1, 26; Jerry Ballinger, "Policy House Closed After 3-Hour Siege," *Cleveland Plain Dealer*, May 24, 1957, pp. 1, 11.

2. "5 Now Held in Bombing of King's Home," *Cleveland Plain Dealer*, May 21, 1957, p. 26.

3. Ibid.

4. Ibid.

5. Jerry Ballinger, "Policy House Closed After 3-Hour Siege," *Cleveland Plain Dealer*, May 24, 1957, pp. 1, 11.

6. Trial transcripts of Petitioner's trial in the Court of Common Pleas, County of Cuyahoga, State of Ohio, as included in Record No. 236 of the Supreme Court of the United States, p. 45.

7. Ibid., p. 46.

8. Ibid., p. 31.

9. Jerry Ballinger, "Policy House Closed After 3-Hour Siege," *Cleveland Plain Dealer*, May 24, 1957, p. 11.

Chapter 2

1. Fourth Amendment to the Constitution of the United States of America.

2. Richard L. Perry and John C. Cooper, *Sources of Our Liberties*, 3d ed. (New York: American Bar Foundation, 1959), pp. 418–421.

3. Ibid., p. 421.

4. Ibid.

5. Ibid., p. 422.

6. Ibid., p. 304; William S. Holdsworth, *A History of English Law*, Vol. X, 4th ed.(Boston: 1938), pp. 667–668.

7. Ibid., p. 132; John Wigmore, *A Treatise on the Anglo-American System of Evidence*, Vol. VIII, 3d ed. (Boston: 1940), p. 281.

8. I Annals of Congress 439 (1789).

9. *Boyd* v. *United States*, 116 U.S. 616 (1886).

10. Ibid., p. 633.

11. *Weeks* v. *United States*, 232 U.S. 383 (1914).

12. Ibid., p. 398.

13. Ibid., p. 390.

14. Ibid., p. 393.

15. Eugene Ehrlich, *Amo, Amas, Amat and More*, 1st ed. (New York: Harper & Row, 1985), p. 79.

16. Ibid.

17. Ibid., p. 42.

18. *Wolf* v. *Colorado*, 338 U.S. 25 at 33–39 (1949), Appendix, Table I.

19. Ibid.

20. Fourteenth Amendment to the Constitution of the United States of America.

21. *Wolf* v. *Colorado*, p. 27.

22. Ibid., pp. 30–31.

23. *Rochin* v. *California*, 342 U.S. 165 (1952).

24. *Irvine* v. *California*, 347 U.S. 128 (1954).

25. *Rochin* v. *California*, 342 U.S. 165 (1952).

26. Ibid., Appendix, Table I.

27. Ibid.

28. Ibid.

29. *Burdeau* v. *McDowell*, 256 U.S. 465 (1921).

30. *Olmstead* v. *United States*, 277 U.S. 438, 485 (1928).

Chapter 3

1. Grand Jury Indictment of Dollree Mapp in the Court of Common Pleas, County of Cuyahoga, State of Ohio, as included in Record No. 236 of the Supreme Court of the United States, p. B.

2. *Martindale-Hubbell*, Vol. II, 89th ed. (Summit, N.J.: Martindale-Hubbell, Inc., 1957), p. 2007.

3. *State* v. *Lindway*, 131 Ohio State 166, 2 N.E. 2d 490, cert. denied, 299 U.S. 506, 81 L.Ed. 375, 57 S.Ct. 36 (1936).

4. Trial transcripts of Petitioner's trial in the Court of Common Pleas, County of Cuyahoga, State of Ohio, as included in Record No. 236 of the Supreme Court of the United States, pp. 7–8.

5. Ibid., pp. 45–46.

6. Fred W. Friendly and Martha J. H. Elliott, *The Constitution: That Delicate Balance*, 1st ed. (New York: Random House, 1984), p. 133.

7. Opinion of the Supreme Court of Ohio, *Ohio* v. *Mapp*, as included in Record No. 236 of the Supreme Court of the United States, pp. 91–92.

8. Friendly and Elliott, p. 138.

9. Brief of Appellant to the Supreme Court of the United States in *Ohio* v. *Mapp*, Record No. 236, p. 18.

10. Brief *Amici Curiae* on Behalf of American Civil Liberties Union and Ohio Civil Liberties Union in *Ohio* v. *Mapp*, Record No. 236, p. 20.

Chapter 4

1. *Martindale-Hubbell*, Volume II, 89th ed. (Summit, N.J.: Martindale-Hubbell, Inc., 1957).

2. Trial transcripts of Petitioner's trial in the Court of Common Pleas, County of Cuyahoga, State of Ohio, as included in Record No. 236 of the Supreme Court of the United States, p. 5.

3. Ibid., p. 16.

4. Ibid., p. 18.

5. Ibid.

6. Ibid., p. 62.

7. Ibid., p. 64.

8. Opinion of the Supreme Court of Ohio in *State of Ohio* v. *Mapp*, as included in Record No. 236 of the Supreme Court of the United States, p. 91.

9. Ibid., p. 93.

10. Ibid., p. 94.

11. Appellee's Motion to Dismiss or Affirm and Brief in Support in the United States Supreme Court, p. 13, as included in Record No. 236 of the Supreme Court of the United States.

Chapter 5

1. Fred W. Friendly and Martha J. H. Elliott, *The Constitution: That Delicate Balance,* 1st ed. (New York: Random House, 1984), p. 138.

2. Audiotapes of oral arguments before the United States Supreme Court in State of Ohio v. Mapp, Records of the National Archives.

3. Ibid.

4. Ibid.

5. Ibid.

6. Ibid.

7. Ibid.

8. Ibid.

9. Friendly and Elliott, p. 141 (quoting an interview with Dollree Mapp, June 21, 1983).

10. Friendly and Elliott, p. 141 (quoting Potter Stewart, "Who Freed Dollree Mapp?" Harlan Fiske Stone Memorial Lecture, April 26, 1983, p. 4.)

11. Ibid.

12. *Mapp* v. *Ohio,* 367 U.S. 643, 651 (1961), citing *People* v. *Cahan,* 44 Cal. 2d 434, 445, 282 P.2d 905, 911 (1955).

13. *Mapp* v. *Ohio*, 367 U.S. at 657.

14. Ibid., p. 659, citing People v. Defore, 242 N.Y. 13, 150 N.E. 585 (1926).

15. Mapp v. Ohio, 367 U.S. at 659.

16. Ibid., p. 660.

17. Ibid., p. 648 (quoting Holmes, J., *Silverthorne Lumber Co.* v. *United States*, 251 U.S. 385, 392 (1920).

18. Ibid., p. 674–675.

19. Ibid., p. 676.

20. Friendly and Elliott, p. 132 (quoting an interview with Carl Delau, June 7, 1983); Telephone interview with Carl Delau, October 20, 1995.

21. Ibid., p. 142; Telephone interview with Dolly Mapp, January 3, 1996.

22. Ibid.

23. Telephone interview with Dolly Mapp, January 3, 1996.

24. *Wong Sun* v. *United States*, 371 U.S. 471 at 487–488 (1963).

Chapter 6

1. *Chimel* v. *California*, 395 U.S. 752 (1969).

2. *United States* v. *Ross*, 456 U.S. 798 (1982).

3. *Warden, Maryland Penitentiary* v. *Hayden*, 387 U.S. 294 (1967).

4. *United States* v. *Calandra*, 414 U.S. 338 (1974).

5. Ibid., p. 354.

6. Ibid., p. 347.

7. *Immigration and Naturalization Service* v. *Lopez-Mendoza*, 468 U.S. 1032 (1984).

8. *United States* v. *Havens*, 446 U.S. 620 (1980); *Walder* v. *United States*, 347 U.S. 62 (1954); *Oregon* v. *Hass*, 420 U.S. 714 (1975).

9. *Michigan* v. *DeFillippo*, 443 U.S. 31 (1979).

10. *Nix* v. *Williams*, 467 U.S. 431 (1984).

11. *United States* v. *Leon*, 468 U.S. 897 (1984).

12. Ibid., p. 921.

13. Ibid.

14. Michael S. Serrill, "A Matter of Good Faith," *Time*, July 16, 1984, p. 57 (quoting Associate Attorney General D. Lowell Jensen).

15. Ibid. (quoting Atlanta District Attorney Lewis Slayton).

16. *Arizona* v. *Evans*, 115 S.Ct. 1185 (1995).

Glossary

amicus curiae brief—A document filed by an individual or organization (such as the American Civil Liberties Union) who is not a party to the case but who has an interest in the outcome of the case. *Amicus curiae* is a Latin term meaning "friend of the court."

brief—A legal document stating the facts and legal theories of a party's case.

case-in-chief—The main portion of a party's case during which it presents its own witnesses and evidence.

clearinghouse—A business where illegal gambling bets are placed and winners are paid.

dissenting opinion—A written opinion by those Justices who disagree with the majority court ruling.

due process—A legal concept that establishes procedures to insure an individual's rights and liberties in all legal proceedings.

evidence—Information consisting of testimony of witnesses, documents, or tangible objects, that tend to prove the prosecutor's or defense attorney's case. The judge presiding over the trial determines whether the evidence is admissible, that is, whether the jury will be allowed to hear or see the evidence. Evidence can be either direct or circumstantial.

exclusionary rule—A rule of law providing that in certain circumstances unlawfully seized evidence—evidence that is seized in violation of an individual's Fourth Amendment rights against unreasonable searches and seizures—is inadmissible in state or federal criminal trials.

fruit of the poisonous tree—If unlawfully seized evidence leads a police officer to other evidence, that secondary evidence is also inadmissible. For example, if the police unlawfully search a suspect's home and find a key for a safe deposit box, any incriminating evidence the police may find inside the safe deposit box is the "fruit of the poisonous tree" and inadmissible at trial.

grand jury—A group of citizens summoned by the government. The group hears the testimony of witnesses and examines evidence in order to determine whether there is probable cause to believe a crime has been committed and that the suspect is the person who committed the crime.

impeachment—An attack on the credibility of a witness who testifies at trial. For example, a witness may be confronted with his or her prior criminal convictions during cross-examination. This is done in an attempt to convince the jury that the witness is not a truthful person.

incorporation doctrine—A legal theory used by the United States Supreme Court. It applies the Bill of Rights to the states through the due process clause of the Fourteenth Amendment.

independent source doctrine—A legal concept providing that evidence that is discovered wholly independent from unlawful police conduct is admissible at trial.

inevitable discovery rule—A legal concept providing that unlawfully seized evidence is admissible at trial if the evidence would inevitably have been discovered by lawful means.

nolo contendere—A plea in which the defendant neither admits nor denies the charges against him or her.

petition for writ of certiorari—A legal document that must be filed by any convicted defendant who wants the United States Supreme Court to hear his or her case.

policy paraphernalia—Gambling slips and records.

probable cause—Sufficient reason, based on existing facts and circumstances, to believe that a crime has been committed or that a certain person committed the crime, or that property is evidence of the crime. Probable cause is a required element for a legal search and seizure.

prosecutor—Attorney who represents the state or federal government in criminal proceedings.

reasonable doubt—The standard for determining whether a person is guilty of committing a crime. In all criminal prosecutions the government must prove each and every element of an offense "beyond a reasonable doubt."

warrant—A legal document authorizing a law enforcement official to take some action. For example, a search warrant authorizes a law enforcement official to search for particular items; an arrest warrant authorizes the arrest of a suspect. In order to obtain a search warrant, a judge or magistrate must find that law enforcement officials applying for the warrant have probable cause to believe the thing or place to be searched contains evidence of a crime. In order to obtain an arrest warrant, a judge or magistrate must find that law enforcement officials applying for the warrant have probable cause to believe that the person to be arrested committed a crime.

Further Reading

Alderman, Ellen, and Caroline Kennedy. *The Right to Privacy.* New York: Alfred A. Knopf, Inc., 1995.

David, Andrew. *Famous Supreme Court Cases.* Minneapolis, Minn.: Lerner, 1980.

Habenstreit, Barbara. *Changing America and the Supreme Court.* New York: Julian Messner, 1970.

Jenkins, George II. *American Government: The Constitution.* Vero Beach, Fla.: Rourke, 1990.

Lewis, Anthony. *Gideon's Trumpet.* New York: Random House, 1964.

Lowe, William. *Human Rights: Blessings of Liberty: Safeguarding Civil Rights.* Vero Beach, Fla.: Rourke, 1992.

Rehnquist, William H. *The Supreme Court—How It Was, How It Is.* New York: William Morrow, 1987.

Ritchie, Donald A. *Know Your Government: The U.S. Constitution.* New York: Chelsea House, 1989.

Sexton, John, and Nat Brandt. *How Free Are We? What the Constitution Says We Can and Cannot Do.* New York: M. Evans, 1986.

Index